THE SMALL TOWN INVESTOR

Real Struggles, Real Freedom, and Real Estate.

by Dave Drew

BWD Capital Publishing (2025)

TABLE OF CONTENTS

Dedication
Introduction
Chapter 1 Welcome to the Shit Show   1
Chapter 2: What's The Point?   8
Chapter 3: Hitting Rock Bottom   13
Chapter 4: The Lie of Someday   19
Chapter 5: Why Real Estate is The Best   28
Chapter 6: Why Real Estate is Not the Best   34
Chapter 7: Finding the Deals!   40
Chapter 8: Analyzing Deals   54
Chapter 9: Finding Money   63
Chapter 10: Wholesaling & Off-Market Deals   69
Chapter 11: Partnerships   79
Chapter 12: Flipping Houses   85
Chapter 13: Vacation Rentals   94
Chapter 14: Buy and Hold Rentals   100
Chapter 15: Property Management   107
Chapter 16: Delegation   115
Chapter 17: The MIB Airport Traveler   124
Chapter 18: Tenant Management   129
Chapter 19: Single Family Houses   140
Chapter 20: Development   149
Chapter 21: Financial Independence   162
Acknowledgements   167
About the Author   168

DEDICATION

*To Diana, Davey, Colin, and Jesse: No matter what,
I am always with you, in your hearts.*

INTRODUCTION

This book began as a way for me to chronicle my personal journey through what was, at the time, a new adventure through the world of small-town real estate investing. Writing down my experiences was a therapeutic way for me to cope with stress, work out solutions, and test strategies. Throughout my first ten years of investing in real estate, I took great pains to try to be the best I could at it. My goal was to achieve financial independence and create something better than what previously existed in our small community. I had many successes and many failures along the way, but I did reach that goal.

As I began, I read everything about real estate investing I could get my hands on. Many authors did exactly what I'm doing now, in their own ways. I learned from the mistakes of others, and I followed the advice of those who were successful. I once heard that knowledge is learning from your mistakes and successes, but wisdom is learning through the mistakes and successes of others. I learn from them all, and there are far too many contributors to thank individually, but they all helped me tremendously. I also found that some authors portrayed themselves as having all the answers; the guiding lights of financial and spiritual freedom. I caution against these types, even though I'm sure some of them might be telling the truth. I am not a guru, a sage, or a genius. I am not selling you a course. And rest assured, I will not ask you for more money. This book will not provide you with a get-rich-quick scheme or promise you a passive, work-free income.

Here's what I will do: I'll share my experiences with you, hoping you will learn and benefit from them. What you can expect to receive is the knowledge and wisdom of a highly flawed person who has tried to improve his life. Most of them didn't work, but many did. In this book, I'm sharing the few that fixed my finances and quickly evolved into the vehicle that now helps many other people. The truth is, I stumbled into real estate, almost by accident. Now, after investing for the last decade, my life has improved dramatically.

Take any of what I have to offer and leave the rest. Pass it along to others if it's helpful to you. If you don't finish the book, fine. If you look up the topics that interest you and work for you, go for it. You don't have to get to the end of this book to be able to use it to help yourself.

I know what it feels like to want to be successful and to be at the end of the line with no hope and no plan. I myself was convinced at one point that I was destined for perpetual failure. Yet, I never gave up.

When you start from a point that is lower than anything you could have previously imagined, there are two realities: First, that there is no worse place you can be. Second, that from the bottom, the only direction to go is up! This makes the bottom a great place to start. What's more is that when you have nothing, every time you do have any success, the gratitude can be saturating. This is the feeling I am left with today. When you have seen the world from this perspective, looking up, every day is "extra". And when every day seems like a gift, you can't help but want to share it with others. So here it is. This is me sharing.

Whether you are a property manager, real estate investor, developer, or simply exploring the idea of becoming one, this book will provide you with insight into the pros and cons of managing properties in smaller and medium-sized markets. You can also use it as a launchpad for development and other ventures. If you get nothing else, you'll be able to laugh at all of my misfortune along the road to financial independence.

What began as an attempt to escape the burden of a nearly upside-down mortgage and a quest to find a way out of the nine-to-five job rat race has evolved into a profitable portfolio comprising hundreds of rental units and development projects. Just as the journey of a thousand miles starts with just one step, my real estate portfolio started with one single rental unit.

Real estate investment and property management are not for everyone, but anyone can do it. I'm proof of that. As a business analyst in my day job and a DIY guy on the weekends, I had a few technical advantages, but I quickly discovered that translating those skills from a theoretical business setting to a real-world application is a whole lot different. In this book, I will outline all the things that did *and did not work* for me along that journey.

My goal is to share my successes, not to boast about them. I want to inform you that a regular person can leverage real estate while working a full-time job and achieve financial independence. I'll also share all my mistakes and failures so that, hopefully, you don't have to make them, too. When it comes to being a landlord and property manager, just as with any venture, to do it successfully, you must believe that you can. But I can't give you that belief. All I can do is try to provide the basis for you to find it on your own.

Back when I used to play music in bars, I'd hear guys joking about this saying all the time: "Don't quit your day job!" Becoming a millionaire while working your day job is possible, but whether or not that's feasible for you will be a decision you'll have to come to on your own. Different people, bosses, and careers will play a role. If you do attempt it, it will involve sacrifice. If possible, and if you already have a job and are looking for a side hustle, my suggestion is to keep your day job while you pursue your dream. It was advice I received from other investors early on, not just in bars. Had I quit too soon, I would have missed opportunities related to loans, credibility, and the trust of other investors. Amazingly, long after I needed my day job, I kept it because I started to enjoy it far more. Once I was financially independent, I became ten times more effective at my job. It's amazing what happens to productivity and workplace performance when you remove the fear of being fired or let go.

Becoming a real estate millionaire while keeping a nine-to-five job was not a goal I ever set for myself. I was after financial security. That looks different for everyone. I've had lots of jobs, but the loss of that last one rocked me to my core. In fact, after that, I decided to work ten times as hard to get out of doing any job. Eventually, I no longer needed one. This accomplishment resulted from a combination of hard work, the help of others, and luck.

Managing property has been one of my keys to success in real estate. My objective is to show you exactly how to utilize property management and real estate investment to achieve financial success. I'm from Long Island, and while my investment experience is mainly in smaller towns, these practices can be applied anywhere by anyone.

While small-town real estate investment can undoubtedly be done remotely, I recommend that property managers, especially those just starting, get their boots on the ground as much as possible. At first, it might be difficult to fully appreciate the importance of the property manager's role in real estate investment, but suffice it to say, it is the most critical aspect of buy-and-hold rentals. Let me reiterate: Property management is the key to successful long-term residential real estate investment in any size market. You cannot do without it. If you don't do it well or hire someone who can, your business will probably fail. Can it be done without doing it yourself? Of course.

Even if you hire a great manager, you will still need to manage that manager. It will always be beneficial to know precisely and entirely what that entails. Approaches will differ between the various property types, but whether they're single-family homes, multifamily units, or vacation rentals, one fact remains: Someone will have to be inside those dirty basement areas, handling the clogged toilets, and taking care of your property when you're not there.

All you need to do is be convinced that you have the ability to do this. From there, make the decision and take the necessary action. Simple. By following the suggestions in this book, you will be armed with the information you'll need to make an excellent start.

Let's go!

CHAPTER 1

Welcome to the Shit Show

Before I became a landlord, if you said to me, "shit rolls downhill," I probably wouldn't have argued with you. Yet, from my personal experience, I can tell you that's not always the case. Sometimes, it shoots back up, gets all over the place, fills up the laundry machines, and sort of oozes back toward you slowly, defying the laws of gravity as you watch in horrible amazement. But before you toss this book in the toilet, let me explain why this is so important to me.

Owning rental property can be a fantastic way to generate wealth, but the idea of being a landlord can be daunting. Often, potential investors get spooked by the horror stories and challenges of broken toilets, professional tenants, and evictions. These are indeed facts of life for landlords, so the decision to become one should not be taken lightly. Perhaps you're seeking an opportunity to build wealth or establish a supplemental income stream. Or possibly you have a career and are looking for a change of pace. Maybe you're already a landlord. Not all real estate investors are landlords, but I am.

Over the last few years, through my experience generating multiple types of income streams —both active and passive —I have discovered a straightforward formula that has consistently worked in my business and across all its systems. It always begins with *a belief*—followed by decisions, actions, and results. Rinse, repeat. By following that simple formula, I have been lucky enough to learn how to evaluate each path my business has taken. I also get a much better sense of the direction it will or might take. So, focusing on the first step of the formula—the belief—I will share an experience that led me to pursue real estate investing further.

Ya Gotta Believe!

For me, becoming a landlord was a particularly challenging prospect. Many major obstacles seemed to stand in the way. Dealing with people was usually pretty straightforward, but could I handle conflicts if they arose? And the toilets—how would I handle the damn toilets?

I am a hands-on person. You may not be, but someone must be. That someone can be you, but it is more likely to be an employee or company hired to manage your property. To fully appreciate what it takes to manage property, I suggest you go to those dark basements and consider the reality. At some point, someone in your organization will spend hours down there. It can be a valuable lesson in understanding the importance of a skilled maintenance person. This is also beneficial because it gives you a sense of how the building is being cared for. Anyone can paint a hallway that everyone walks through—but it takes a special kind of property manager to sweep and clean a basement that no one is ever going to see. You're looking for people who care about you, your business, and your tenants.

To become a real estate investor, I would have to participate in investments as a landlord. Before I decided to go "all-in," I experienced a long period of trepidation. Many people quit here. I had heard all the horror stories, but was also enticed by the prospect of creating wealth and making money. Nevertheless, for a long time, my desires were outweighed by my fear. Like any other successful decision in my life, this one had to be predicated on a firm conviction—a belief that I could become a landlord and real estate investor. I wasn't convinced. Not at first.

I needed some experience before the belief could become real. There are many ways to test the waters. Internships, mentor programs, REI groups, books, podcasts, websites, or simply old-fashioned conversations with other landlords and real estate investors are all great ways to advance toward a decision.

I asked myself if others could do this, could I do it too? Did I know everything that would be involved? How would I consider the risks vs. the rewards? Did I have what it took to be a landlord? Could I stomach the challenges and live through the nightmares I had heard from other failed landlords? These and a million other fears flooded my mind as I questioned, not whether it could be done, but whether I could do it.

To clarify, I had a fundamental misunderstanding of what an investment was. I thought you had to be rich to be an investor. When I was growing up, it never occurred to me that investing was a means to create wealth, rather than something only wealthy people did. My experience of living in a paycheck-to-paycheck household taught me that there were no stocks, bonds, or mutual funds to fall back on. Life seemed to consist of getting loans, going to college, getting a good job, and working your ass off for thirty years so that you could retire and then begin to enjoy your life, at sixty-five years old!

The people living in the "rich houses" down the block were not like us. They had great jobs or were left with large inheritances, or so I thought. For my family, the primary focus was the monthly struggle to pay the mortgage and the credit card minimums, all while managing to put food on the table. My parents worked hard, and while we understood the value of money and hard work, we never really learned how to manage our finances or understand them. Throughout my years of schooling, no one ever taught me about money. I only knew that I wanted it. I certainly never learned how to make it work for me. So, because I never thought I could be an investor, I wasn't. Then,

I made a huge mistake.

My family was going through changes. It was growing fast, and my wife, Diana, and I decided to move out of our tiny Cape Cod starter home. We found a unique house that had been on the market for almost a year. The layout was odd, but we thought we could make it work for our growing bunch of (soon to be three) kids. We also thought the layout and its time on the market meant that we might be able to get a good deal. We went for it! As part of the negotiation, I removed the contingency that required us to sell our existing home before purchasing the new one. Contingencies are conditions of the sale. In our case, we thought we could persuade the seller to keep the price low by offering to remove the sale contingency. We thought we could make the financing work if we sold the old house in a month or two. As it was June, the prime home-buying season, I figured it would be no problem. I was wrong again.

Six months later, we were still carrying two mortgages and paying giant bills for our new house. I had refinanced the original thirty-year loan to a fifteen-year loan a few years earlier. The mortgage for the new house, like the home itself, was significantly larger, and the taxes in the new town were triple those of the old place. I hated the idea of renting out our first home, but I disliked it less than selling the house at a price below what it was worth to us. It was our first home together, and we put our hearts and souls into every square inch of it. I have fond memories of sanding the glue off our definitely asbestos tiles long before I knew or cared what asbestos was. The idea of strangers coming in and trashing it made the decision very difficult. Nevertheless, with the holidays and holiday expenses upon us in December, we did the unthinkable. We rented it.

A Day to Memorialize

The rent was $1,300, and that covered the mortgage and very little else. When the water heater went, that pretty much ate the year's cash flow. On the upside, much of the

$1,100 mortgage payment—about $500—was going toward the principal each month. When I looked at it from that perspective, we were making about $700 per month on the rental. That's $8,400 per year. So, although I stumbled into it, I began to realize the potential in real estate ownership and renting. In this case, the advantage of the principal being paid down due to the earlier refinance to a fifteen-year mortgage was huge. I was becoming an investor, and while I could sense that something was starting to change, I wasn't a believer yet. Then I got a call from our new tenants, who were about six months into their one-year lease… on Memorial Day.

In a frantic tone, he said, "Dave! Umm, we've got a problem over here. I didn't want to bother you today, but I didn't know what else to do. We were doing laundry like we normally would, and everything started going crazy. The sewer seems to have backed up, and now there's sewage, like, all over the place and up the pipes into the first-floor shower."

He said it was filling up the laundry machines, sinks, and tubs, and it was all over the basement. I pictured our lovely home entirely covered in someone else's waste. This was the call I had been dreading, and the timing, on a holiday weekend, was unbelievable.

"Okay, man," I said. "I'll see what I can think of and get over there as soon as I can."

I left the family barbecue and headed over.

It sounded awful. I quickly watched a few YouTube videos, borrowed a few tools, and set out. Thanks to my grandfather and my father, I have always been pretty handy, so I figured I'd give it a shot. Because of the holiday, the drain guy wanted $600 to show up. That seemed like a rip-off, so I went to work in the muck.

Snaking, jabbing, and fighting with the sewer clog, it was winning. I couldn't get it. I fought for what seemed like hours. It wasn't budging. I could feel the clog, but couldn't push the snake past that point. I wondered what it was. Roots? Toys? Rocks? I kept at it. Nothing. I put everything down and gave up. As I began to wrap the snake back up, I felt a sense of defeat.

Later, when I reflected on that moment, I realized it wasn't just a sewer line I was contending with that day. It was as though everything I had risked was riding on successfully clearing it—my mortgages, the new house, my family, my job, my decisions, my ego. All I wanted was to push them—and whatever was physically blocking that channel—down the drain. So, I gave up.

Then, it occurred to me that maybe I shouldn't give up. What if I quit now, and only one more try would do it? I had a little left in the tank. Maybe a second wind. So, I went back at it. Then I quit. Then I started again. After a few more minutes, right when I was about to give up for real, again—with the snake all the way extended—lo and behold, I felt something push through! I yelled out, "I gaaahhhht it!!"

It was at that moment, in the basement on Memorial Day with a combination of other people's human feces and urine on my body, that I realized I could do anything! Top of the world! And not long after that, amazing things started to happen.

I was proud of the accomplishment. My tenant, who had been watching me fight with the drain snake for about two hours, seemed impressed. I had more than kept up my end of the bargain, and he knew it. I lectured him a bit about the amount of dog hair that was everywhere, including in the laundry machine, and how that had probably contributed to the issue. He never had a problem, never paid rent late, and always treated me with respect.

After that experience, as I drove home, it occurred to me that if I could do this shit, I could be a landlord. Not only did I have a breakthrough with the drain that day, but I had also broken through the terrible barrier of uncertainty that was between me and my real estate business. Suddenly, I had the belief I was looking for.

Now, unclogging a sewer drain on Memorial Day does not make me a great landlord or real estate investor. The point is that some of us are harder cases than others. Some of us need to delve into the fear and return to the beginnings, where our beliefs lie, to change our thinking and combat the parts of our character that stand in the way of greatness. I had to quit a couple of times before I was successful. For you, this challenge may involve dealing with tenants, securing funding, or negotiating with property sellers. You may be worried about what people think or how you're viewed, or maybe you're simply struggling with confidence. Perhaps you're not bothered by any of this, but odds are, you have something standing in your way. Whatever that may be, I advise using whatever it is as the absolute signpost for the direction you must travel. Courage is not, not being scared. It's seeing the fear and walking into it, especially when you don't know how to do something.

Before that Memorial Day shit show, I did not see the massive opportunity that presented itself right in front of me. Even afterward, it took countless hours of analysis, education, and relationship-building before I took the next step and decided to become a proactive real estate investor. Yes, I decided to invest in real estate; however, I never would have been able to do it had I not started with the belief that made it a reality.

Here's the great news: anyone can have the belief. It doesn't have to take getting covered in shit to know that you can be an investor and a property manager. I already know you can do it. All you must do is believe me. You don't need to know how to unclog drains, evict tenants, collect rent, get loans, or analyze deals. All that stuff comes later. Your real journey will always begin with what you believe to be true at this moment.

CHAPTER 2

What's The Point?

Even if you think you're not ready, you know managing property and investing in real estate can create wealth. You know people are doing it, and although you may still need convincing, you can do it too. Now, if you've gotten this far, it's time to decide something else. We're going to get a bit philosophical here, so clear your mind. Get your candles out, or your yoga mat, or whatever you use to get to a state where you can take an honest look at yourself. It's worth taking the time now to find out a few key things about why you're here.

What is the point? Why do you want to become a real estate investor or manage property? There are lots of other things you can be in this world, and not everyone is suited for this life or this business. Sometimes, we feel like we don't have the luxury of choice. You may think of investors or property managers as wealthy moguls with ample disposable income and yachts. Definitely yachts. Some of us do have these things. But most, like me, do not. I'm just a regular guy with a family who got sick and tired of being dependent on a job for my financial security. To be successful in life, it is helpful to have a noble reason to pursue something. It will increase your chances of success.

I'll share with you how I found my "why" and some steps to help you find yours.

Although I've had some success making tough decisions on my own, I've found that some of the best information sources are others who have made the same decisions. Whether their choices turned out positively or negatively isn't the main point. People with knowledge and experience are helpful. Alone, we can tend to get stuck in what is referred to as "analysis paralysis." We try to figure things out, hedge our bets, and forecast. What's the result? We overthink and underact. I liken my success to a quick quote you've probably seen on a meme somewhere, "Fail your way to success."

I can't tell you how many times I've tried to get good at one thing, then quit—how many times I have started something I thought was a good idea but then failed to make it a reality. College, home improvements, sports, instruments, relationships, food; you name it, I've bungled it.

Most of my failures occurred when I embarked on tasks without a clear end goal in mind. Take any 9-5 job I've ever had, for example. Somewhere along the way, it became clear to me that climbing the corporate ladder was important. Working as hard as I could for someone else's company in an effort to get more responsibility and importance seemed like the goal I should be working for. I just jumped into the race without thinking about the finish line. Rather, I myopically thought of the current leg of the race as the whole thing. I just jumped in somewhere in the middle and started running as fast as I could.

What usually happens when racers sprint at the wrong time? Was I in the right race? Why did I think racing was right for me? In the moment, the stress of the day-to-day work life can be blinding. What many of us see is the Gatorade at the break station. We see the refreshment provided to us for trying so hard, but we fail to understand the point of the race. Is it even a race? I started down a path with no clear sense of where I was going because I had no idea *why* I was going.

Often, we know we want something different, but the

trouble is that it's not precise enough for real success. Maybe you want to escape the pain of your current situation. With negativity as fuel, motivation is temporary. You're dead in the water before you ever get going.

Why Would You Ever Want to Do This?

Author and speaker Simon Sinek wrote a book titled *Start With Why*. He points out that while it's easier to identify how we do things and what those things are, what we tend to either forget or fail to keep in focus are the reasons why we do those things. He contends that success is mainly predicated on our understanding of the reasons why we do things. If we lose focus, forget, or pick the wrong "why," we are far more likely to fail. These reasons must be sound if we are to become successful. Keeping this in mind through our day-to-day lives is paramount if we want to be optimally effective.

Do you know what your "why" is? What drives you toward success? This question can be applied in any area of your life where you want to succeed. If the "why" is noble, serves a purpose, and is well-defined, it passes the test.

For example, saying, "I would like to become a real estate investor and rent houses," does not pass the test all by itself. You know what does? "I would like to become financially independent so that I can provide for my family without relying on a job or a corporation for my security." That was mine, but you're welcome to borrow it.

Once our reasons are established, we can move on to determining what success looks like for us—the strategy, tactics, and goals. We must, however, be deliberate, decisive, and intentional to achieve goals and succeed. But how?

There's a basic system anyone can use. The process begins with "why," but further hinges on our belief that something *can* be done. Once we believe something, it becomes possible. Without a real, true conviction, nothing is possible. There must be a vision followed by a decision and actions. Otherwise, you stay stuck.

Once armed with an idea, a vision has the fertile ground it needs to develop and grow—imagination blossoms. Dreams turn into goals and seem to become attainable. Perceptions can change. Options start appearing.

To get to this point, ask yourself some questions. Check back in on your "why." Is what you're doing aligned with it? Have you jumped into someone else's race? Write down your goals—not what your partner or boss wants, but what you want. Are these ideas consistent with your larger goals? Will you be able to act on them? If so, what is the first step? When will you do it? As long as you take some form of action and commit to repeating it, small advances over a long period of time can yield huge results. As author Robin Sharma points out, after time and repetition, this can become the most powerful tool in your life. Practice this. It may sound simple, repetitive, and even pedantic, but we must consider how we limit ourselves to all kinds of possibilities in our lives, many times before we even get started. I think of these as our upside risks. Don't sabotage yourself before you get the chance to be successful. Make small changes, and if they produce even the smallest positive results, commit to repeating them.

When we were children, we believed we could do anything. People tell us, "You can be anything you want to be!" We believe them. As kids, we wanted to be police officers, doctors, astronauts, and presidents. Of course, some people accomplish those goals, never losing sight of them and fulfilling their childhood dreams. For most of us, though, as we grow, we start to see the barriers to all the things we thought we could do as children. They rise quickly and become excuses, or we listen to the influential people in our lives who tell us we can't. The negative voices begin to drown out the positive ones. Before we know it, we're doing jobs we never wanted and striving for things within our lives that are far departures from what we really want.

What usually happens is that somewhere along the line,

we started paying more attention to the reasons things can't be done rather than remembering how intrigued we were with chasing facets of the world that we didn't understand. Challenges. We forget the exhilaration of wanting to be the president or a firefighter and instead think more about the fear, time, and commitment. We drift away. The dreams fade. Before we know it, there we are again, safely dead in our tracks, having thoroughly sabotaged ourselves.

But here's the good news: you don't have to keep doing this. You can harness the power required to break these patterns. You can do this right now. In fact, right now is the only time you can do it. If you're anything like me, and you've just realized you've been doing it wrong, stop. You can't go back and fix it. You can only fix it now.

CHAPTER 3

Hitting Rock Bottom

When I was twenty-two years old, I drank alcohol every single day. I was living at home (again) after a three-and-a-half-year failed attempt at college. On one particular day, I was passed out, sleeping one off in my childhood bunk bed. I felt a hand on my leg. Someone was grabbing me. It was my dad. Startled, I yelled, "What the hell are you doing?" It was the morning of September 11, 2001. "Wake up," he demanded. "We're being attacked!"

As usual, I had been up all night partying at a local spot on Long Island with whoever would still hang out with me. Since my return home from college the previous winter, I'd been on an extended bender for almost a year. The job they let me keep at the catering company required that I show up at around 4 or 5 p.m., which I could handle at the time. The partying had been out of my control for several years, but I was nowhere near ready to stop. I drank for six more years after that, and it didn't get any better. Dangerous, damaging, and at times suicidal, I could never seem to see a way out—not a safe one, anyway.

Sometimes, I wish I could portal back into that kid's head to see what things looked like. It's not like he understood what he was doing to himself or others around him. Even if I went back in time and told him personally, that kid wouldn't have changed. He simply wasn't ready, and it definitely hadn't gotten bad enough. He was the one being attacked, and unbeknownst to him, he was also the attacker. That's how his illness worked. So, what made him stop, and what makes the bottom so different for so many? Why do some "have it" and others only seem like they have it and don't? Some never stop. Some never try. Loads and loads die.

If you talk to a sober alcoholic or drug addict who's been that way for a while, they'll probably tell you that they thought they hit bottom before they truly did. The stories can be very different and range from hysterically funny to horribly tragic, with everything in between. If you listen long and hard enough (or if you just believe me), what you'll inevitably notice is that bottoms are different for everyone. We don't have to become a homeless drunk or even a drunk at all. These bottoms can come in many forms: divorce, bankruptcy, behaviors, illness. I've watched people gamble away their savings in casinos and the stock market. I've also seen them throw away marriages, families, and health. You name it. Many of us do have to get to the point where the consequences of our actions are so unbearable that we cannot continue. My experience was with alcohol and drugs, but humans can use anything to destroy themselves.

When I was twenty-six years old, I still drank alcohol every day, still. My whole life had become consumed with drinking, planning to drink, and what I still called "partying." Once in a while, I did something so stupid, horrible, or dangerous that I'd wake up the next day and think I was ready to quit.

Maybe after next weekend, I'd think. *Maybe after the next party or trip or concert happens.*

Horseshit. All of that.

Eventually, a particularly bad episode ended with my arrest. I had completely alienated my friends, my wife, and several completely innocent people. I had broken the law, and I deserved the consequences I was about to receive.

Why does this keep happening to me? I thought.

I really had very little understanding of the fact that I was causing all of the problems that I had in my life. After about ten thousand dollars and a plea deal, I stopped drinking for about a month. A whole month.

Somehow, I managed to land a management position in the company I worked for. Alcoholics are funny this way. If they show up for work, they are often very dedicated, hard-working, talented people. I was that guy. I could turn the focus on when I needed it. I could tap into my work ethic, charming character, or undying need to please other people and get into or out of almost anything. Add a bit of booze and some like-minded work associates, and I climbed the ladder very quickly. Before long, I oversaw six regional offices and 350 employees. I'd show up some days and have to lock myself in an office because I'd been up all night and smelled terribly of booze. I was hungover and worried all the time.

Scared, nervous, and totally unable to stop, I had zero control over whether I was going to drink. Then, when I started, I had no control over what was going to happen or what I was going to do. I ended up in all sorts of tragic places and situations, having no idea how I'd gotten there. Arguments, fights, and a lot of drunk driving were near-everyday occurrences. Sometimes, I wished I just wouldn't wake up after the blackouts. Facing the things I had done had become unbearable.

With my life intact on the outside, I had a wife, a house, and a car in the driveway. I hadn't lost it all, but I knew I was going to. I'd sit on the barstool and tell people all the things I was going to do with the rest of my life, but deep in my heart, I knew it was all a lie. Travel, projects, family … that stuff was never going to happen. What was really going to happen was that I was going to jail, or I would die a horrible alcoholic death. So, what do you do when those look like the only choices? There were no good choices. I could never stop, and I'd inevitably hurt all the people I loved so much. I decided the world would be better off without me. I'd have to kill myself. When I came to, I was in the back of a paddy wagon on the way to jail. The officer told me that the guy next to me, the huge naked one, had killed two people that day. I looked around at my "fellows" and realized something. This is where I was going to be for the rest of my life.

After they let me out of jail that morning, I went back to the hotel and lay on the bed. I called my wife on the phone, and with tears in my eyes, I said, "I think I might need help." You may say this all the time. I say it all the time now. But back then, I never said that. Never.

That was eighteen years prior to this writing, on the morning of September 11, 2007, the day I finally surrendered.

That's what the bottom looked like for me. There has never been another day that looked the same. It changed everything. If you asked that kid about that day back then, he would have told you that it was the worst day of his life. If you asked the man that kid has become, he'd tell you it's more like the best day. The fact is, I wouldn't trade it for anything.

Everything that came after that day I consider to be "extra." As a result of that surrender and the actions that followed, I have been given a life filled with immense gratitude and immeasurable joy. My family, my friends, my business, and most of all, my freedom have been gifts. I was trapped in a jail that I put myself in. Today, I can use that experience to help others, but only if they want to be helped. In hindsight, there was help out there, but I couldn't seize it until I was ready. I couldn't ask. I learned that hard work and willpower were the indispensable assets I could leverage to get what I wanted. When they inevitably failed, I was lost.

Here's the good news. You don't have to be at rock bottom to ask for and receive help. For a long time, though, I found it nearly impossible. It was unimaginable to be vulnerable. There were many times around those years when I was looking for a quick way out of debt, a way out of relationships, and sometimes, a way out of jail. There were other times when my habits and behaviors led me to the point of total disaster and destruction. I was hurting people around me, taking wherever I could and trying to avoid doing the thing I knew I had to do to stop.

In many ways, I no longer blame myself 100 percent. What happened to me, what I did to myself, was the same thing millions of people have done. I was addicted. Hooked on alcohol, drugs, and risks. You name it, I wanted more. Different people can maintain this type of lifestyle for varying lengths of time, depending on their stamina and degree of pain. Some endure unimaginable pain for decades. Others fast-forward through decades of abuse in just months. The thing that happens to most addicts, alcoholics, and high-risk-takers is that, at some point, they are unable to continue their progressively worsening behavior at the rate the addiction or alcoholism is pushing them to.

When this happens, they usually hit what is referred to as rock bottom. For me, after years and years of abuse and destruction, I had reached that point. There was only one way I thought I could escape. Whatever your defects may be, it doesn't have to go this far. I thought of all the things I couldn't control. All the people I was going to let down. All the problems I thought I would never be able to resolve. Money, jobs, relationships, all of it. It snowballed. It was too much. I can still feel myself exploding inside, hitting the gas, and when that van was going as fast as it would go, I jerked the wheel as hard as I could to the right into the trees. I wanted oblivion. But that's not what I got. I got everything else.

The day after a suicide attempt might look like the worst day of your life. At that moment, to me, it certainly did. But I found it also provided me with something I didn't have before: perspective. Like George Bailey on Christmas Eve in *It's a Wonderful Life*, I got to consider what the world might be like if I were no longer in it. The day after I survived, I didn't feel the same way. I have come to believe that there was no other path for me. I had to do it exactly the way I did it. I apply this to suicide, my life afterward, and, yes, even later in my real estate career. I dealt with all the feelings of loss, pity, and shame. Eventually, I started to see that the way I was living my life was not the result of the world being against me. It was the result of my being convinced that the world revolved around me. This was the exact opposite of reality, and when I couldn't see anything for what it really was, I didn't believe I had a choice. Never thought I could stop. But I did. The power of shifting from self-destruction to self-improvement is like a slingshot. The catalyst is hitting bottom long before the beliefs, decisions, and actions are made.

My experience with inebriation and my subsequent sobriety and the years that followed my suicide attempt may seem far removed from you. But is it? Can't we all relate to personal battles, failure, and loss? Challenges that seem bigger than they might be. The light that follows some form of darkness in our lives. We all have our own individual struggles. Some are more pronounced and visible than others. Many suffer quietly. Our defects can seem more treacherous than they are, but ultimately, if we can see beyond them, the goal of getting better and improving our personal situations really is universal and available to everyone. This book is designed to show you that anyone can do what I've done—in real estate, business, or personal matters. My belief when I was twenty-eight years old and hopeless was that I was also useless, used up, and undeserving of a place on this side of the grass. So, when I saw others accomplishing so much, so young, a part of me thought it was too late. Never listen to that voice. It's not too late. You're not too old. You're not all washed up.

You can still change everything.

CHAPTER 4

The Lie of Someday

I used to tell everyone about all the great things I was going to do someday. I spoke of adventures and accomplishments I would undertake—someday. Often, I even imagined myself doing those things, being in those situations—someday. But there was one giant missing piece: the decision. I never actually decided anything. At times, I pretended I would do things just so you would like me. Deep down, I knew I was always going to be stuck. Sounds depressing, right? It was.

The result of a life spent wishing for things instead of deciding to do them feels terrible. Here's the bottom line, just like Creedence Clearwater Revival says: "Someday never comes." Someday is an absolute lie.

If we sit around waiting for things to happen, they *will* happen...*to* us. These might be bad things. Wouldn't you rather make decisions and enjoy the fun that comes from acting? Trying and failing is far better than never having tried at all. At the end of the day, you know you can go *back* to the drawing board and try again.

The point is not to waste time waiting, deciding, and analyzing just because you don't know *how* to do something. Nobody knows *how* to do something before they start. We don't know anything until we decide to do it and then take action. If you can't swim, read a book about swimming and then jump into a lake. Let me know how that goes. No, you must get your hands dirty as quickly as possible if you want to accomplish anything new.

"But Dave, I don't know how to do it. What if I lose money? What if I fail?" Well, losing money and failing are two of the best ways to learn.

Let's explore this a little more. Maybe you'll decide you want to be a pilot. You might read every single book there is about being a pilot. You could totally understand aerodynamics, physics, and the scientific reasons humans can fly. You might know the material so well that you could even teach it to someone else. By all accounts, you'd know how to fly. But, until you jump into the cockpit and give it a go, you'd be mistaken.

Don't give yourself a chance to quit before you get going. Get into the pilot seat and start flying as soon as you can. It's ok to be a co-pilot. Whatever it takes, start taking action. Apply this principle to your job, your business, your marriage, your family, your hobbies, and your health. All of it!

A Formula for Success

Step 1: Identify your why. If you want to do something and you have a goal, it will pay to analyze the reason you are setting the goal. Write it down. Discuss it with other people whom you respect and trust. Discuss it with those who have experience in the field. Say it aloud. If it's noble, helps others, and is rooted in something you love, you are on the right track.

Step 2: Define your belief. Write it down. Talk about it with those who have experience. Say it aloud. Decide if you believe you can do it. Have others done it? Can you be passionate about what you're chasing? Is it worthy of your time? What will it help you with?

Step 3: Make a decision. Say it aloud. Then ask someone else to help keep you accountable by checking in with you about it from time to time. Just having a thought is different from making a decision. When you decide, things change. Your thought patterns, your mindset, and the actions that follow define it.

Step 4: Take action. Any action. Baby steps are fine. You will make mistakes, but remember that we fail so that we can succeed. Identify the components of your goal and break them down into manageable steps until they are completed. You only go up. Otherwise, you go down. You must keep moving. Success requires intensity and focus. Stop hesitating and start making things happen. If you fail, go back and try again. Never give up, and you can never truly fail. Pivot, adjust, and get back in the saddle.

Step 5: Measure results. Analyze what worked and what didn't. Consider what adjustments are needed to achieve the desired results. Evaluate the actions you've taken and determine if you're satisfied with the current results. If you are, rinse and repeat. If you are not, go back to step one and reevaluate your why. Have you made it earnestly? Is it steadfast? If not, change it and start again.

Decide to Be Successful

At one point in my life, I was thrown away. A boss told me, "Dave, we're going in a different direction, and we've decided we no longer need you to work here." I was seeking something to replace the insecurity I felt after losing my job as a manager in a large corporation. During a coincidental conversation with a coworker, she mentioned she had several rental properties that she was able to buy, rehab, and manage, all while keeping her day job. I was intrigued. She was not what I thought a landlord looked like.

I had a rental, but only because I couldn't sell it for what I thought it was worth. I had not considered that I was already doing what she was doing—unintentionally. She mentioned a website that gave her some insight into getting started. The Bigger Pockets website had a podcast that she said might also be helpful. I began listening to the Bigger Pockets podcasts and buying the books and products the commentators and guests discussed. Turns out, real estate was more than interesting. It was thoroughly fascinating to me.

I loved the strategies, the creativity, and all of the options. The flexibility of the deal was always an exciting driver. What I loved most about it was the possibility that it might be a solution to my problem. This was the answer to my why! The means to my end. I wanted to be financially independent, but it always just seemed so far away and too much work. Additionally, I often felt like I was too late. If others were having success, I was probably starting too late in my life. Pay attention to these lies and see them for what they are—fear in disguise.

In the books, talks, and videos I started voraciously consuming, I listened to others sharing familiar, similar, and sometimes the exact fears and experiences as mine. I began to believe this could also work for me. Many of them were just like me. I identified and related to them. If they could do it, maybe I could too?

"Once you make a decision, the universe conspires to make it happen."
— *Ralph Waldo Emerson*

Working for a large corporation, I liked my job, and I thought the work I was doing was a good representation of myself. I had a staff, and we had staff meetings. I had a boss, and he had staff meetings too. I had colleagues whom I liked and some whom I didn't like. It was all very standard and normal, I thought. Well-respected in my field and with a strong reputation, I was also well compensated for my services. I've always been a diligent worker, and I strive to excel in my endeavors. I worked for years for the same company in the same industry and still had a passion for what I did. I was highly skilled, and I taught other people those skills. I traveled extensively and enjoyed the places I visited and the people I met. Then, one day, my boss called me up and told me I was going to be laid off.

It's a familiar story, and it's happened to millions of people, but it was new to me. It was horrifying. One minute, my life was humming in a particular direction; the next, everything changed. That's how life is. I spent the next month looking for a job, crying, yelling, and floundering around, wondering what was going to happen to me. It was kind of messy and humbling, and it was all the other things that go along with the feeling that you've been thrown away for no good reason. And that was it. There really was no good reason. I was doing a good job, people liked me, and my work product was good. The company was just going in a different direction. After the requisite stages of denial, anger, etc., I eventually made it to acceptance.

One night, while I was yelling at the Mets on TV for something they were or weren't doing, it occurred to me. Why not start my own business? I had friends who had done it. I was smart and accomplished, and I had some valuable skill sets that I could bring to the table. Of course! This was what I'd do.

I proceeded to research everything I could on starting up a business in New York. It looked expensive, but I kept at it. Years ago, someone dear to me had an idea that seemed to make sense for the market I was in at the time. They suggested I start a laser tag/recreation business. There weren't any around, and the market was ripe for recreation-based businesses. As a child of the eighties, I remember how cool laser tag looked when I was a kid. I knew it must be way different and so much cooler now. Back in 1985, I got a laser tag set. These black space-age guns with red lasers on the sides were fascinating to my sister and me.

That was going to be a great Christmas. The best!

I had a business idea, and everything I read said I should write a business plan and start preparing my pitch to secure the $130,000 in start-up funds for the equipment and the $100,000 in commercial real estate space I was going to need. I continued researching and talking to laser tag equipment companies and property owners, still having no idea how I would fund (or run) my business. Then, in June 2016, a gunman attacked Pulse, a popular LGBTQ nightclub in Orlando, Florida, in one of the deadliest mass shootings in US history. The tragic event claimed forty-nine lives and left more than fifty others wounded. That day, my whole perspective changed on the idea of promoting my business. I wasn't going to be able to stomach it. It wasn't in line with the way I lived my life. The timing was just off, and it wasn't a fit for me. The main theme of my business, shooting, had lost its appeal. I was out of business before I began. Was it a failure? Maybe, but maybe not.

I thought about the conversations I had with many of the real estate investors with whom I'd discussed the commercial property. While I had no genuine interest in that area of real estate, I did have a single-family residence (SFR) that I'd been renting for a couple of years. I wondered if that income stream was one I could expand on. My SFR was several years into a fifteen-year loan, and most of my rental income was going toward equity and cash flow. It seemed like an opportunity, albeit a slower-moving one than I had originally envisioned.

I began searching real estate sites - just for fun. I didn't have much cash, so I figured there wasn't much I was going to be able to do right away. After a while, looking through the local multiple listing service (MLS), I started to get a feel for which properties were priced attractively and which ones were overpriced. Having had some success with my SFR, I was looking at cheaper versions of the 4Br/2Ba Cape in similar areas. I would only need about 20% down, a mortgage, and a passing credit score to make a small deal. I thought it was possibly doable.

I knew a few people who were real estate investors, but

for whatever reason, it seemed like they always complained about it. They said things like, "It's a hard road to travel," and "Get ready for dirtbag tenants to clog your pipes and ruin your houses." Some of those landlords looked like they'd lived hard lives and seemed awfully jaded. You know, like maybe at one time they were happy and then got the idea to be landlords, and that ruined their lives? Anyway, I'd already been through some disaster property management stuff, so I pressed on.

After a while, I started to see the properties through a new lens. It seemed like another perspective change was revealing itself. Instead of thinking the stench of the places was repulsive, I started to think that they might smell like opportunity. Holes in the walls weren't bad things. My ability to fix them made them good. Wrecked carpets were a chance to replace and give some first-time renters a comfortable living room. I had been up and down my first primary residence and redone everything, so at this point, I was comfortable with most minor updates. Plus, I was starting to establish a network of colleagues, contractors, fellow investors, and groups of folks who were willing to help. I started attending a local Real Estate Investor (REI) meetup and began to source different financing options. This was really going to happen. Before I knew it, the answer to my first strategic question (could I stomach this market?) was yes. Not only could I stomach the market I was getting into, but I was going to leverage and harness its disadvantages to provide great housing to great people. That's when I knew I was going to get into action.

Getting Into Action

Analyzing deals on paper by night and looking at tons of houses by day was my only job for a while. I began to research Home Equity Lines of Credit (HELOC). This was my solution to the start-up problem. I wasn't going to get a Federal Housing Authority (FHA) loan, which is designed for lower-income borrowers and meant for people who are going to owner-occupy.

I didn't have the time or the promise of a paying job that would allow me to sit around and save up. Through good fortune, timing, and luck, I got another job, but I kept at the learning and the research. I didn't give up. My goal was to become financially independent, and I finally took the next step and made the decision to get there.

From there on out, it's been all action. I went to the bank and inquired about a Home Equity Line of Credit (HELOC). I worked with the mortgage broker for a while, and she guided me through the process. I provided my income details, along with all my balances on things like credit cards and car loans. Then, she started talking about something she called DTI. She explained that DTI, or the Debt-to-Income ratio, was a calculation banks use to determine whether a borrower is a good risk and whether the borrower would be able to pay back the debt under all circumstances. They're always optimistic when you walk in the bank door because they want to sell the loan. It's what they do. It can be intimidating, but especially at the beginning, it's an extremely valuable effort. Not only are you starting a relationship with a lender, but you're also learning the process of borrowing—and maybe later—of lending money. In the end, the loan officer explained that while I had a significant amount of equity in my house, once they looked at the DTI, they could extend me a line of credit of $75,000. It wasn't the $200,000 that I was looking for, but it was enough to make a start. Not long after that, I started making real offers to buy. Before I knew it, one was accepted. I negotiated a good deal, and once again, perspective struck. How was I going to manage these tenants I was about to be responsible for?

There I was, presented with a possible solution to my problem. I knew it could be done, but I just didn't know if I could do it myself. Was I on another precipice of failure? Another aborted idea that couldn't leap the hurdles of fear, worry, and anxiety? Was the pain I was experiencing going to block my way, or would it become so bad that I made a change? Pain is good for that, you know. For change, it's a signpost. It points back to the path I need to be on. I use it to tell me when something must change.

This time just seemed different. The gears were turning, and the goals and opportunities were shining brighter than the multitude of reasons not to do it. I spent what felt like months doing real estate deals on paper, analyzing. I could have lost it, but I took steps to remind myself why I was seeking this goal. I never forgot that feeling of being thrown out of my job. I knew financial independence was key to my family's success, and I knew that an REI business that ran well could solve problems for other people, too. So, I pressed onward.

CHAPTER 5

Why Real Estate is The Best

Real estate cannot be lost or stolen, nor can it be carried away. Purchased with common sense, paid for in full, and managed with reasonable care, it is about the safest investment in the world."

— *President Franklin D. Roosevelt.*

If real estate is not your only business, I wouldn't blame you. But if it's not some part of it, I would. If you choose, real estate can be your only business, too. It is such a unique investment vehicle that we need to discuss some of the best reasons to focus energy on it. There are dozens of advantages, but I'll list the primary reasons.

Appreciation

Over the long term, real estate tends to appreciate in value. At the macro level, I suggest investing in markets that are appreciating or expected to appreciate, assuming all other factors remain equal. A cash-flow, value-based investor is different than a speculative investor, or someone who bets on things like market appreciation. A deal must be good on paper, without factoring in appreciation rates, for me to consider it. Speculation sounds like guessing, and while there is a lot to appreciation-based investing, it doesn't resonate with me, especially as a newbie. With every dollar at stake, you may be looking for something as close to a sure thing as you can get. This is why appreciation should be considered as the proverbial icing on the cake. If it happens quickly, great. If it doesn't, it's still great! The bottom line, though, is real estate will appreciate, but not always at the speed or at the exact time when we wish it would. It's slower, can suffer downturns, and while not as volatile as something like a stock price, it will steadily improve in market value over a more extended period.

One more note on appreciation. For the buy-and-hold investor, while appreciation is the icing on the cake, the role it takes when coupled with cash flow and leverage is exponential. One of the coolest things about real estate is that there are so many ways to make money. If you were to take each piece, each ingredient on its own, you could still make money with any of them independently. But, properly combining all the ingredients: cash flow, leverage, and appreciation, combined with a good chef (or property manager), you'll have the secret sauce you need to become very wealthy.

Cash Flow

Cash flow is a key benchmark factor for most investors and a prerequisite for conducting a positive buy-and-hold real estate analysis. As a buy-and-hold investor, you plan on holding an asset for a long time, at least over one year, but probably more like five to ten years and beyond. Depending on your strategy, you may use mortgages to leverage property or hold the asset as equity without any loans. In either case, cash flow is essential.

Before considering almost everything else, examining cash flow pro formas is the first gate through which a good deal must pass. In its simplest sense, the question is: Based on reasonable and conservative assumptions, will this investment property generate net monthly income?

If you are buying a house for $100,000, you can do some quick calculations. A super-fast method is the 2 percent rule. Can you rent a $100,000 house for 2 percent of its purchase price, or $2,000, per month? If yes, you are probably going to be okay. If not, proceed to the next step. What are your expenses? What is your mortgage payment, if any? Plug them in: Rent minus Expenses minus Mortgage Payment equals Cash Flow.

Here is an example of a house that cash flows well:

Annual Property Operating Data						
Sale Price		$100,000		100 Main St		
Units	2	Sq Feet	3,200			
Rent 1	1000	Rent 4		Rent 7	Rent 10	
Rent 2	1000	Rent 5		Rent 8	Rent 11	
Rent 3		Rent 6		Rent 9	Rent 12	
Income				Financing		
Total Gross Monthly Rent		2,000	Loans	Amount	Int%	Term
Gross Scheduled Income (Annum)		24,000	1st Loan	70,000	7.00%	30
- Vacancy	8.33%	2000	2nd Loan	0	4.00%	30
+ Laundry		0	Total Debt Servicing			
+ Other		0	Loan Amount			70,000
- Other		0	Monthly Principle			0
Gross Operating Income		22,000	Monthly Payment (PI)			466
			Annual Payment (PI)			5,589
Operating Expenses			Initial Investment			
Taxes	0.00%	2,700	Down Payment			0
+ Insurance	0.00%	1,200	+ Loan Points	0		0
+ Property Mngt	0.00%	1,100	+ Closing Costs			3,000
+ Advertising	0.00%		Initial Investment			73,000
+ Repairs/Maint	0.00%		Depreciation			
+ Accounting/Legal	0.00%		Depreciation Basis	79,000		2,873
+ Water/Sewer	0.00%	800	+ Additions			0
+ Fuel Oil	0.00%		Depreciation			2,873
+ Electric	0.00%	0	Taxable Income			
+ Lawn Care	0.00%	300	Net Operating Income			14,900
+ Gas	0.00%	1,000	- Mortgage Interest			0
+ Janitorial	0.00%		- Depreciation (bldg.)			2,873
+ Trash removal	0.00%		- Taxable Expenses			6,000
+ Telephone	0.00%		- Amortized Loan Points			0
+ Optional	0.00%		+ Bank Int Earned			0
Total Expenses	0.00%	7,100	Taxable Income			6,027
Cash Flow Before Taxes			Cash Flow After Taxes			
Net Operating Income		14,900	Cash Flow Before Taxes			9,311
- Debt Service		5,589	Tax Bracket %		28.00%	1,688
- Additions		0	Cash Flow Per Month			635
Cash Flow Before Taxes		9,311	Cash Flow After Taxes			7,624
Investment Highlights						
Price Per Sq. Ft		$31.25	LTV			70.00%
Price Per Unit		$50,000	Break Even Ratio (BER)			6.87%
Capitalization Rate		14.90%	Cash on Cash Return			12.76%
Debt Coverage Ratio		2.67	Rent/Value			2.00%

Leverage

One of the other wonderful things about real estate is that it can be leveraged. You can borrow money against its equity. Equity is your ownership percentage of the real property. For example, if you put $20,000 down on a house worth $100,000, your equity in the property is 20%. Let's look at a quick example of how leverage can work when considering your equity in a property. Let's say you bought in a market that was appreciating rapidly. Property values are increasing because more people want to live in the area. Best case, you do nothing, no renovations at all. Before you know it, houses just like yours are selling for $140,000. You may think that because you only put $20,000, your equity has shrunk. In fact, it's the opposite. It's gone up! You now own the original 20 percent, plus the appreciation. Your original investment of $20,000 is now worth $60,000, or 43%. If you wanted to refinance your mortgage, usually up to 80% of the the appraised value of the house, or in this case, $112,000, you could pull out more cash that you originally paid. Equity and leverage together constitue unrealized and therefore nontaxable gains that you can borrow against.

Leverage almost always factors into your real estate portfolio, especially when scaling up. Leveraging using mortgages, private money, and hard money lenders are the best ways to get from a few rentals to a lot of rentals. The key to proper leverage is, of course, cash flow. You want your investments to be able to pay your debt and maybe put a few bucks in your operating accounts. If your investments are just enough to pay your mortgage, this is okay because you are also paying equity within every mortgage payment. There are as many types of debt and borrowing options as the mind can come up with, but the most common in real estate is the mortgage. There's a reason for that.

Tax Advantages & Depreciation

Real estate has yet another advantage when compared to other asset classes. Not only can you generate cash flow from your investments while leveraging them, but you'll also see another huge advantage when it's time to do your taxes each year. Even if you failed your cash flow analysis, overpaid on a deal, and got wrapped up in a mortgage with tough terms, the US government values real estate investments so much that it allows you to deduct your losses from your taxable income. That's not even the best part.

We covered appreciation—which is your property increasing in value based on economic factors such as supply and demand—but depreciation is the basis the government uses to value and deduct the cost of buying and improving real estate from your taxable income. In a nutshell, if you spend money to buy and improve real estate, you have to spread those costs out over the life of the investment, but you also get the benefit of deducting the entire value of the asset over 27.5 years from your taxable income, too! In the above example, you can see that $2,873 is the amount you would deduct on the purchase of a $100,000 rental house in one year. This is reduced from the amount of money you have to pay taxes on. This is like the cherry on top of the icing on top of the cake.

Another tax advantage (maybe the best) of buying and selling real estate is the 1031 exchange. This is also referred to as a like-kind exchange. A 1031, or like-kind exchange, is a part of the tax code that was implemented over one hundred years ago. 1031s can be used to defer taxes on gains made from selling real estate. The idea is that you sell a property, and then within the next six months, you replace it with another property of like-kind. The IRS allows an exception to the tax law using code 1031, and defers the gains until you sell the property you replaced. You can continue the 1031 process and defer the gains as many times as you want.

There are entire companies built upon this one tax code section. They are known as Qualified Intermediaries, or QIs. Because of the significant advantages provided by the 1031 and the strict rules the IRS makes you follow, QIs are also held to firm standards of operation. While most of them do not take very much responsibility for how you handle the exchange, there are many that I've used that are fantastic. Some of the downsides to 1031s are that they can be mishandled, have time frames attached to their handling, and if you are under pressure to provide a replacement property to save on taxes, you may make a hasty real estate purchase decision. There are entire books on 1031s, and while they are not a big part of this particular book, two companies that I've worked with successfully are Legal1031 and RJ Gullo Company, both out of New York.

Providing Great Homes

Perhaps the best part of real estate investment has nothing to do with money. Knowing that you provide clean, safe places for people and their families to live can be highly and unexpectedly rewarding. This feeling is compounded when the great tenants you are housing are coming from unstable or unsafe places. Maybe they're marginalized, disadvantaged, or simply at odds with their life situations. While great tenant screening and rigorous processes are required to house people in property you own or manage, human situations are simply part of the deal. If you are compassionate and empathetic, you will be highly rewarded when you find you are able to help people. This can, of course, backfire, because it will hurt when things don't go so well. But, if you keep good processes intact and stick to a strong business plan, the number of people you'll be able to help by providing housing will far outnumber the corner cases

DAVE DREW

that don't.

CHAPTER 6

Why Real Estate is Not the Best

When my business was small, I spent more time screening, talking to, and meeting my applicants. As my business grew, I shifted my personal focus away from this piece. It was a huge mistake. If you are a buy-and-hold investor renting to the public, you should design a robust system for your application process. Today, we conduct background checks for criminal and credit history, speak with references, contact each former landlord, and require documentation of paid rent. Despite our best efforts and refined processes, all designed to minimize risk, we still encounter unfavorable tenants.

When we start to realize a tenant is going south, we reach out to them immediately. If it's a payment issue, we attempt to reach an agreement for them to settle the payment. If they fail to make the payment within the agreed-upon timeframe, we will not wait to initiate the nonpayment eviction process. I used to wait longer and give people the benefit of the doubt, but the fact is, it costs us little to take the first step here in New York, so we serve notice and demand rent in fourteen days. If they do not keep their promise, we keep ours. We move forward to the next step, which is to get a court date.

If the reason the tenant is struggling is not related

to rent payment, it may be a nuisance, garbage, or noise issue. Here, we follow the local laws on serving notices to cure the violation. We serve the notice, wait for the required timeframe by our municipality, and then recheck the issue. If it's not resolved or cured, we move to evict them. While I am compassionate, understanding, and empathetic, many of these issues do not get to my desk. If they did, I'd likely make the same mistakes I've made in the past. I've designed this system to correct my own personal weakness. It may sound strange to hear that I developed systems to circumvent my emotions, but understanding your weaknesses will certainly make you a better business leader.

At the end of the day, I am a business owner, and the responsibility that comes with that means I need to do what's best for the business. That doesn't always align with my feelings. Bad tenants, whether they are non-payers or rule breakers, have the power to put others at risk. From financial risks to safety risks, it's incumbent upon the responsible business leader to prevent these people from harming those around them, to whom you've also pledged responsibility. Don't forget that. When your emotions say, "Let's give him another month," what you might be doing is prolonging the pain of one of your employees, tenants, or partners.

Dealing With Officials

When I first started in the real estate investment business, I was naïve. Not only did I fail to set my goals high or big enough, but I also harbored preconceived (and incorrect) notions of what might happen as my business scaled. At the closing of my third investment house, the seller stressed to me the importance of speaking with the Code Enforcement Department and the Refuse Department to inform them of the new ownership so they would know where to send future violations. I thought, what? Why would I, the greatest new landlord on the scene, ever need to talk to the Code Enforcement Department? There would surely never be an issue with my properties that would involve a code violation! Well, she was right, and I should have called.

There were no issues happening at my third rental property, but eventually, there would be. My goal that day was to get in front of these. It's a very simple step, and it goes a long way because no one else is doing it. Call your local municipality and ask to speak to the Code Department on the phone. Ask them some questions about best practices, and make sure they know your name. This can seem counterintuitive, but trust me, it works. The next thing you want to do, if you can spare the time, is to meet with them. Walking into a local mayor's office and meeting with local officials is priceless. Personally, I enjoy doing it, and it serves to let them know that my business and I will stand out from the rest.

I cannot tell you how many things get easier when the people in local offices and municipalities like you. You're not there to bribe anyone with your ass kissing. You're there to be human, to acknowledge their existence and effort, and to begin to put names to faces. Relationships—all sorts—are the number one way to be successful in business. Building strong relationships with local officials in your town or municipality will always be a huge source of relief, especially when you encounter problems, and if you do this for long enough and scale to almost any degree, you will encounter problems. That's what we do here. We solve problems.

Utility Bills

You want to talk about being powerless? There's nothing more crushing than going to the post office box on water bill day, opening the envelope addressed for what you thought was a great producing asset, and realizing that a toilet must have been running for four months. That entire years' worth of profitability has been literally flushed down the drain. I still dread that giant stack of water bills and the gut-dropping fear that I endure while opening them.

You may not have such fears because you live in an area where water is priced reasonably. But water and energy prices are insane for most of my investment property. This is what happens when government bureaucracy decides how to correct their bullshit mistakes. It's a longer story, but you may be experiencing something similar in your neck of the woods.

Basically, our local government hired a company with an over-bloated contract to build a new water treatment facility. The project went over budget by tens of millions of dollars and was overdue by years. Corruption seemed rampant. Lots of people got rich, and then the facility failed and had to be rebuilt! No one involved paid the price for the multimillion-dollar mistakes. What ended up happening is that the sewer bill rates for everyone in the region doubled and have never gone back down. They never will. Today, a toilet running for just one day can cost about $35. Couple this with the fact that our antiquated meter and billing systems have no alerts and accrue charges over four-month billing cycles, and you can see how one running toilet can lead to a $4,000 water bill. It's an absolute travesty, but it means that property owners have to find solutions.

After paying over one hundred thousand dollars in water bills for things that definitely do not constitute regular usage, we've had to spend time, money, and effort developing systems aimed at protecting us from overages. This extends to energy bills, such as gas and electricity, as well. The tenants are the first line of defense. You might think that if a tenant leaves the toilet running and or runs the heat when it's warm out, you can just charge them for the overages. First off, not many tenants in low-to-middle-income rental apartments have an extra thousand dollars lying around, nor are they willing to admit their mistakes. In addition, in a multifamily apartment building, it's nearly impossible to prove whose fault something like this is, and even more challenging to assess the real value of it. It's a dead end.

Instead, we send our team out to read meters on a regular basis, count the numbers, do the math, and when we see something anomalous, we start to investigate at the unit level. We've had a lot of success here, and while we're hopeful that new water monitoring systems, smart meters, and technological advances furthering conservation will be in place someday, a responsible landlord and investor cannot wait around for systems to fix their business. They must act.

Depending on the system you are involved with, of course, all municipalities are different, and this may or may not be an issue for you today, but it probably will be someday. Water, our primary resource supporting *our way of life*, is precious. Conserving resources will not only help your business, but it will also help the world. I like helping the world, so we do our part to stress to our residents how valuable these resources are. Nothing is perfect but our tenants seem to be getting the message. We start with them, stressing things like our inability to keep rent rates down when we face such high energy and water usage issues. From there, we convey the same message to our maintenance staff. From the top to the bottom, from owners to staff to tenants, we are aligned in our efforts to save energy, water, and money. As the world changes, water and energy conservation and usage will become more of an issue. We want to be ahead of that curve.

Black Swan Events

Given the serious nature of the COVID-19 pandemic, Black Swan events have to be a part of a business's risk protection strategies. They cannot be ignored. Many of us are independent business owners and investors as our main source of income, and now that many of us have been through a major one, we have to keep these experiences fresh in our minds. From a financial security standpoint, black swan events such as COVID-19 and its business impact were quite serious. During the COVID-19 pandemic, as my partners, colleagues, and fellow real estate investors met and spoke, we knew one thing. The businesses that survived the pandemic were going to be the ones that were successful in the long term.

Many days during the COVID years seemed like all we could do was try to get to tomorrow. Thankfully, my family stayed relatively safe from the sickness, but they endured all the stress—the effects of government regulation, job market failure, and financial strain—put on us. If you were a landlord or property owner from 2020 to 2021, you know what I mean. If you were not, well, take it from me - it was an impossible time. The horrible part of this particular "black swan" event was that it moved so slowly and seemed never-ending. It was less a black swan event and more an ice age-long, sun-drowning glacier of dead black swans that overtook a world we never thought could be so dark. Even at the time of this publishing, the far-reaching effects of the COVID-19 nightmare are still unfolding, but we were right: those who endured remain. My advice to anyone going through an event like this is just to keep going.

Have you ever noticed that real estate investors seem to be active no matter what is going on? If interest rates are low, they're refinancing and getting new money mortgages. Have you noticed that even when interest rates are high, they're still investing? How is this? Well, go back to the ingredients in the cake. Because real estate factors are appreciation, leverage, and cash flow, with property management holding it all together, investors are actually better insulated than most against even the worst tragedies that occur in society. Whether it is the financial crisis and subsequent recession of 2008 or the COVID-19 pandemic, as real estate investors, we didn't give up. We pushed through, and during the low times, we leaned on our management and diverse portfolios. During the high times, we looked for ways to make our money work for us and to invest in intelligent ways. Let's make something clear. Investing and betting are two very different things, but you always have to consider that something could happen that no one expects. Following specific guidelines is great, and you should always do what works for you and your business, but remember, when the going gets tough, don't quit. That's the only way to really fail.

CHAPTER 7

Finding the Deals!

If you want to be a real estate investor, you must be able to find deals. There are certainly a lot of methods to do this, and while no one way is the only way, it will depend on what suits you the most. Figuring out how to manage your deal flow will probably start with looking at your strengths and weaknesses. You may be more inclined to leverage technology and AI. Maybe you are more old school and have a talent for personal interactions. Whatever you decide works best for you, keep this step at the forefront of your business. Let's start with the basics.

Driving for Deals

Have you ever driven around the neighborhood and noticed that there are houses that don't seem like they fit? Growing up, we neighborhood kids always knew the houses on the block that were vacant because we were intrigued by them. Some weren't vacant, and we feared the people who might be inside them. Before I became a real estate investor, I would have said something like, "Man, somebody should do something about that place!" Well, that somebody turned out to be me, and now that somebody can be you!

The first thing I do today when I see one of those houses is write down the address. They're all over the place. They don't have to be totally shot, either. The worst house in a nice neighborhood may not be that bad, but it could be great. There may be a reason they're not fixing the roof or never mowing the lawn. Those reasons can often be the tip of the iceberg. You'll never know unless you ask.

In these situations, I start with the property records. You can usually find these online, though some districts will charge you for access. A quick search will point you in the right direction, and if you are already familiar with the market, that's a good starting point. If you can't find the property owner online, before paying for access, I suggest calling the local municipality and asking for assistance. This is how we used to do it in the old days, before machines took over. Once you have the mailing address of the owner, you'll already know more than most people. It is important to note that you would usually expect the owner's mailing address to be different than the physical address. This indicates that the owner doesn't live in the house. If the mailing address is the same as the physical address, you will likely have to keep digging. Search for the owner again and see what other addresses are available. Depending on what you find, try to reach the owner by phone. Text or call and let them know that you're interested in purchasing their property. If they are not the right person to speak to, try to find out who is. Don't be pushy, and always be respectful. Also, be transparent. I can't stand it when I get calls from sketchy salespeople, especially when they immediately start asking me all sorts of personal questions.

The Lost Art of Letter Writing - Yellow Letters

If you can't reach the owner by phone, there is a tried-and-true method that has worked for investors over and over. Get a yellow legal pad and write the owner a handwritten letter. I still do this today. If there are just a few, or one, I write them myself.

I bought my first flip this way, so I know it works. Include your phone number, your email address, and why you're writing the letter.

Here's the exact template I use:

> Dear Mr. Smith,
>
> My name is Dave Drew, and I am a local real estate investor here in Broome County, NY.
>
> I am interested in buying your house located at: 123 Main St., Anywhere, NY 12345.
>
> If you are interested in selling your property, there are many options we can discuss.
>
> I am available by phone, text, or email, and I can be reached any time.
>
> Please contact me directly to discuss options.
>
> Thanks!
>
> Dave Drew
> (607)-555-5555
> bwdcapital@yahoo.com

Once you've got your letter template together, track them on a spreadsheet so you have a record of what you've sent. Decide on the number you can send and sign, stamp, and mail! I do about twenty to thirty at a time, but there's no rule. It's as much as you can handle. If you listened to Grant Cardone in his book, *The 10X Rule*, which you should, he'd tell you to figure out a comfortable number, then multiply it by ten. I agree. Action and more action. If nowhere else, that's where you'll find your competitive advantage. Of course, you can get a virtual assistant or hire someone to write the letters for you. There are also dozens of companies that compile lists that contain property data that is joined with information not commonly found in property records.

Driving for deals can be a great way to start contacting potential sellers, getting inside houses, and building the relationships you're going to need to be successful in your market. The best thing you can learn as a beginning investor is how to find deals. While driving around the neighborhood can be fun and interesting and lead you to great deals, it does become time-consuming, and the return on that time does not always materialize into deals. To cast a wider net, if that's what you're trying to do, you may want to start using larger volumes of direct mail.

Direct Mail Campaigns

As I outlined in the template, yellow letters are direct mail letters you send to homeowners, letting them know you would like to buy their property. As I mentioned, when driving for deals or whenever I write any letter by hand, I always use a standard-sized yellow legal pad. There's probably some marketing science behind this, but for me, I just like the way the blue ink looks on the yellow paper.

To save time and effort, a company I have used in the past is Yellow Letters Complete, www.yellowletterscomplete.com. There are a lot of companies that provide letter-writing services, and at the time of this writing, they cost about $2-$3 per letter. For this, you get a printed letter in ink and a font that resembles handwriting, mailed inside a handwritten envelope. I still think handwritten letters are best, but if you want to send a lot of letters out, this could be a good solution. The best part about the service that sends letters is its ability to combine property owner records with other data. You can do this on your own, but it can be quite labor-intensive.

Where I live in upstate New York, organizations like the

Department of Motor Vehicles (DMV) collect information as a natural course of their processes. What you may not realize is that the DMV, as well as many other institutions, like your bank, credit card company, and phone application creators, are capturing your data and selling it. Personally identifiable information (PII) is becoming increasingly protected, but we often share it without consent. We voluntarily provide this information as we consume products. Think about those long lists of terms and conditions you never read, but always check the box for. Chances are, you've authorized companies to gather and sell your information to anyone they choose.

Property records don't require the same things driver's licenses or credit cards require, so by purchasing lists with a few different pieces of information, companies like Yellow Letters Complete can aggregate them and point them toward real estate investors. I'm sure you can see how this would be useful. I've tried varying sets of criteria for filtering, and in each market, both the options and applications may be different. For example, a real estate investor looking for multifamily properties doesn't want a list of single-family homes, but a house flipper would. A wholesaler may not want to differentiate them. Depending on what type of investment you are doing, this is what will determine your target market. When flipping houses, consider the following criteria:

- Owner Age—55+. Owners in this age group may be ready to sell and relocate.
- Time of Ownership—10+ years. A long period of ownership often means substantial equity and possibly a landlord ready to sell.
- Pointed Zip Codes—Focus on the five closest to your target area. This approach helps you make localized decisions.
- Absentee Owner—This identifies landlords and owners who do not reside at the property. It's based on discrepancies between property records and actual addresses.

- Equity—The percentage of equity indicates the extent of mortgage payment completion.

Yellow letter companies purchase lists in various localities and then aggregate them with publicly available data. They can also buy access to public records online. As a result, they can provide buyers with specific criteria about potential sellers, narrowing the list of mailers they send out. Targeting your market makes your letter campaign far more efficient than broadly mailing everyone in a zip code. It is also significantly more cost-effective. I have probably conducted half a dozen letter campaigns in the last five years, and the results have been tremendous. If I send out one hundred letters, I can expect to receive about thirty phone calls in the first two weeks. More will trickle in even years afterward. From those initial thirty calls, I will analyze every deal on paper first. After that, I will probably go and look at five to ten of them. Out of the five I see, I will probably make offers on all of them and secure one or two deals per one hundred letters. Not a bad return rate, in my opinion, for about $200.

The Hidden Value of the Yellow Letter—Meeting Deb

The best part of these campaigns has not been the deals. It's been the people, the other investors, and the future partners I've met through the process. Think about it. If you target absentee owners, you're automatically including other landlords, property managers, and investors. These are the people who are doing what you want to be doing. If you've targeted owners based on a specific criterion, chances are you'll tap into an expert knowledge base.

When I first started to meet owners who were thinking about selling their houses, many of them were intrigued by my process. They wanted to know about what I was doing, where I got the ideas, and whether the initiative worked. You can gain a fantastic wealth of information from these types of discussions: best practices, pitfalls, and basic wisdom from people who have already had their 10,000 hours in. What's more, many of them were on their way out of property management but had not fully divested. I wondered what an exit strategy from the rental business would look like, and before I considered what these folks were doing, I was presented with seller-financed opportunities, land contracts, and business partnerships.

Four months into my fledgling real estate investment career, I launched my first direct mail campaign. That's when I met Deb, a woman who owned a modest house; she was considering selling. She called me on the phone and we agreed on a time to meet at the property.

As we toured the dilapidated property, I could see the extensive work it needed—foundation, drainage, water service, and more. Standing in the midst of the mess, I shared my story with her. "I was almost out of a job once," I began, brushing aside cobwebs as we walked. "Lost nearly all my financial security. Now, I want to restore homes like this one and provide better living spaces in communities that desperately need it." She listened, nodding slowly as we stopped inside what used to be the living room. "That's quite the vision," she remarked. "You really think you can turn this place around?" "I do," I assured her. "With some hard work and a little faith, I believe it's very possible." She paused and looked at me. I couldn't tell if she was sizing me up or simply wondering why I seemed so excited about the broken-down hovel we were standing inside of. Something happened I can't describe well enough. Almost like something bigger was there guiding this all along… Alas, by the end of our conversation, as we stood there in the fading light, she agreed to sell me the house at a great price. The next day, she surprised me again with another phone call.

"Would it help if I held the mortgage for you?" she asked.

"That would definitely help," I replied, hardly believing my ears.

Before closing, we even negotiated the financing for

another property she owned. As it turned out, she had like a hundred houses! I've since refinanced one of those deals, and our relationship has blossomed, resulting in many other mutually beneficial opportunities. Deb is an amazing person and one of my very close friends today. I never would have met her had it not been for all of the other chances I took leading up to that meeting.

All this from a single yellow letter and a genuine conversation. In a subsequent chapter, I'll delve deeper into the value of building relationships and partnerships. While it's possible to succeed alone, cultivating strong relationships is by far the best way to expand and enhance your business.

Direct mail may seem antiquated, I know, but consider your audience. It may seem like an old-school method for seeking deals because it is. That's what people like about it. It takes work to write a letter and then to pick up the phone and discuss the deal, your business, and even yourself, but in my experience, those are the ways you gain the trust of your seller, and that gets you deals.

Real Estate Agents

One of the themes of my success has been to use the knowledge of people who have it and are willing to pass it along. Think about it. If you are an expert at something, you've perfected your craft and figured out how to achieve success over a long period of time. You've truly created something to be proud of. I am always trying to identify these people. They can be invaluable resources, especially if they want to share their knowledge. Many do. They simply want to share what they know. Is it free of charge? Maybe not, but it can be worth the price, most times.

I know many real estate agents; while most aren't

investors, those who are can be precious. These agents understand the market deeply, offering insights into retail purchases and market analytics. In return, they typically seek loyalty, hoping you'll choose them to list and sell your properties.

The trouble with real estate agents and real estate investors is that they do different things. As luck would have it, I met a realtor who had been in the business for thirty years at the time. I learned more in that first meeting with him than I did by reading half a dozen books. Then, when he showed me a few calculations, and I saw the numbers he presented on the screen in his office on a simple spreadsheet, I knew I was going to be able to start analyzing deals.

Agents often have specialized market knowledge, which can be crucial, especially for new or remote investors. However, remember that you're not obligated to remain loyal to an agent unless you explicitly agree to it through a contract. While building mutual relationships is valuable, be aware that agents can sometimes overstep. Maintain focus on your business goals and remember that your interactions can have a significant impact on your growth, particularly in smaller communities.

REI Meetups

Another great way to build relationships with local investors, potential partners, and vendors is through local meetups. These can be referred to as Real Estate Investor Associations (REIAs) but don't have to be formal at all. The local Chamber of Commerce, Rotary Club, business groups, trade organizations, and real estate boards are all great places to meet like-minded people who work in related fields. I've done all kinds of deals that stemmed from meetups just like this.

Young Chris

After attending a local meetup I was invited to, I met

Chris, a young man who clearly did his homework. He didn't seem wealthy yet, but his enthusiasm for real estate was exceptional. He also possessed experience that I lacked. In his mid-twenties, Chris had already completed several house flips and was the joint owner of a few dozen rental units. He was invested in trailer parks in Pennsylvania, and though I think that venture was mostly a relative's, he shared considerable knowledge and wisdom at his early age. He was about twenty-five, and his experience genuinely impressed me.

Chris loved sharing the knowledge he had while running the REI group in our small county. The meetings were monthly, and it was a physical place for local real estate investors to show up and just talk about what they were doing. The vibe was always positive, and the investors in the group were very helpful to one another. I'm not sure it's always like that because competitiveness and egos tend to budge their way in when you start talking about money and influence. But this was never political, not really. Instead, it was collegial.

The way Chris set up the meeting was cooperative. He would hold the meetings in the back of a large local diner. Each person who wanted to order food or drinks could do this at any time. That way, the group didn't have to cover the expenses. For the first forty-five minutes or so, everyone would talk casually and mix about projects they were working on. People would share contact info and sign in, and you could always see little relationships budding. It was a great way to start the meeting.

Next, Chris would have a speaker present to the group for a little while. Maybe thirty-five or forty more minutes, or less. The speaker was usually someone local who partnered with real estate investors. The nice part about this speaker presentation was that it gave local businesses the opportunity to present themselves to a group of people who were spending money locally and expanding the housing community. Housing providers are usually a frugal group, but they can obviously be extremely valuable partners. There were investors in that room who had one rental unit and others who had hundreds.

The impact the meetups had on my early investing career was intense. One activity the group facilitated was a go-around-the-room session where investors introduced themselves and gave their "elevator pitch." If you're not familiar with what that is, picture yourself on an elevator ride with someone who just asked, "Hey, what do you do in your business?" You get the length of the ride to give them an overview of what you do.

My first time, I said this:

"Hi, my name is Dave, and I am a real estate investor mainly interested in buy-and-hold rentals with flips on the side to generate cash. I currently own and self-manage five rental units on the South Side. I'm interested in increasing my portfolio to twenty units by the end of the year. I'm looking for financing, partnerships, and ways to share any knowledge I have."

There was something powerful about saying that aloud. It was the first time I actually heard myself say those words. Someone once said that if you want to be something, say it out loud, and that will be your first step toward knowing you can and will do it. Saying, "I am a real estate investor," made it more real for me. Try it.

Social Media

Social media outlets are excellent examples of low/no-cost advertising channels. Using your own social networks is often the first avenue to create awareness around what you're doing. A friend once told me the best way to get a new job is to tell people you're looking for a job. The best way to find real estate to purchase is by telling people you're looking for real estate to purchase. If you are not comfortable mixing your real estate aspirations with your personal social media contacts, you can easily create separate profiles, pages, or groups to spread the word. When it comes to putting the word out, start small and go from there. In terms of advertising on social media, the algorithms will gladly accept your money. You can dial-in these ads over time and with a bit of focus, get excellent results. It appears everyone has a podcast, is a content creator or leverage social media to promote their brand. I do not, but it seems to work for people, so maybe someday...

Websites

Using personalized websites like www.thesmalltowninvestor.com is a tried-and-true method for capturing information on potential sellers. With minimal setup using sites like Wix, Bluehost, or Ionos, you have a plethora of options. The nice thing about having a site like this is that you have a link you can post or send anywhere. It goes on your emails, your social media, and your business cards. You can easily send it to your contacts and update the site's look and feel without needing assistance. Alternatively, you can also use more complex solutions designed specifically for real estate purchases. In my experience, low maintenance, low cost, and high data capture rates are key. I prefer to collect rent, not pay it to internet companies every month.

Business Cards

If you're going to be a real estate investor, get a business card. Hand them out to people, put them up in diners, and use them in all of your business meetings. Vistaprint is the option I've used for years, but there are, of course, a million options. One thing to keep in mind before you order too many: As you scale, you may need to change your contact info, so keep that in mind before ordering one million business cards.

Newspaper Ads

When I was a kid, there was a guy on late-night TV infomercials. He was always saying, "I make thousands of dollars from my tiny one-bedroom apartment, and all I have to do is place tiny, classified ads in newspapers!" It turned out, Don

LaPre was a scam artist who eventually committed suicide while awaiting a court date, so there's certainly more to it than just placing the ads. If you think about who reads newspapers these days, you may consider that this could be a target market for you. Most newspaper readers are online subscribers, and while the days of people reading tiny, classified ads are ending, online, subscriber-based papers still target higher earners and educated people. Furthermore, given the online medium, it has become easier to both target an audience and use digital advertising as a means to get your message out there.

Bandit Signs

Ever see those "We Buy Houses" signs on the telephone poles while you're waiting at a red light? If you haven't noticed them, take a look. They're there. Bandit signs are among the oldest tricks in the Real Estate Investor's playbook. They're referred to this way because you're not supposed to put signs on telephone poles. Bandit signs have a phrase and a phone number on them. Call one and see if you know the guy. They may have a deal for you. Sometimes, it's a more complex operation; other times, it's the small-town millionaire next door. Bandit signs are a great, low-cost way to get the phone ringing, which is what you need.

Online Meetings

Online REI groups are a quick way to gather information. I'm part of dozens of social media groups that are excellent conduits to other real estate investors. Sites like BiggerPockets.com have evolved from their humble beginnings but remain extremely helpful. Essentially, any forum where like-minded individuals discuss similar topics can be a great source of knowledge.

After some time, you may find that you possess

knowledge others seek. Whether you're a beginner or a seasoned investor, sharing your insights with those starting out or those with different experiences can be rewarding—one of the ways you can give back. It's not just about competition and making money. I look forward to reaching out and enhancing others' know-how every day.

Humility in Business

One of my weakest skills was building relationships. By nature, I can be a very self-centered person. I want you to like and appreciate me, so I go to certain lengths to prove to you that I am good enough. I didn't always know I didn't have to do this. We all have character defects. This is one of mine. I'm sure it's thwarted me in ways I don't even know about. One of the greatest things about the meetups was that I could get out there with others and learn, share, and also realize that there are always much bigger fish. There are always people who are smarter, richer, and more experienced than me. If there were so many in my small town, there must be a lot more elsewhere. For someone like me, and you may be nothing like me, I needed to find some humility. This didn't mean that I would lower my goals. In fact, it did the opposite; it helped me increase my goals and get to where I wanted to be a lot faster. We'll go deeper into building relationships later.

CHAPTER 8

Analyzing Deals

One of the best tools in my investor tool belt is a simple rental calculator. As was covered earlier, my first exposure to this tool was through the first real estate agent I ever called about rental properties. His name is John, and he opened my mind to the numbers behind deals.

Rental property analysis is a must-have skill for any investor but for the new investor, it's a skill that needs to be honed. Back-of-the-napkin math will work, but probably not until you've looked at dozens or hundreds of deals. If you don't know how to do it, you can easily make big mistakes. I still use the basic rental calculator I developed to fit my needs, every day.

The Rental Calculator

You can find it here: www.thesmalltowninvestor.com

Annual Property Operating Data			
Sale Price	$100,000	Address	123 Main St
Unit Details and Rent Info			
Total Units	3	Sq Feet	3,200
Rent 1 $500	Rent 4	Rent 7	Rent 10
Rent 2 $700	Rent 5	Rent 8	Rent 11
Rent 3 $575	Rent 6	Rent 9	Rent 12
Income			**Financing**
Total Gross Monthly Rent	$1,775	Loans	Amount / Int% / Amort
Gross Scheduled Income (Annum)	$21,300	1st Loan	$24,000 / 9.00% / 20
- Vacancy	8.33% / $1,775	HELOC	$0 / 3.25% / 20
+ Laundry	$0	**Total Debt Servicing**	
+ Other	$0	Loan Amount	$24,000
- Other	$0	Monthly Principle	$0
Gross Operating Income	$19,525	Monthly Payment (PI)	$216
		Annual Payment (PI)	$2,591
Operating Expenses			**Initial Investment**
Real Estate Taxes	42.69% / $3,316	Down Payment	$12,000
+ Insurance	12.87% / $1,000	+ Loan Points	0 / $0
+ Property Mngt	25.13% / $1,953	+ Closing Costs	$1,000
+ Advertising	0.00% / $0	Initital Investment	$100,000
+ Repairs/Maint	0.00% / $0	**Depreciation**	
+ Accounting/Legal	0.00% / $0	Depreciation Basis	$60,000 / $2,182
+ Water/Sewer	19.31% / $1,500	+ Additions	$0
+ Fuel Oil	0.00% / $0	Depreciation	$2,182
+ Electric	0.00% / $0	**Taxable Income**	
+ Lawn Care	0.00% / $0	Net Operating Income	$11,757
+ Gas	0.00% / $0	- Mortgage Interest	$0
+ Janitorial	0.00% / $0	- Depreciation (bldng)	$2,182
+ Trash removal	0.00% / $0	- Taxable Expenses	$5,816
+ Telephone	0.00% / $0	- Amoritized Loan Points	$0
+ Optional	0.00% / $0	+ Bank Int Earned	$0
Total Expenses	100.00% / $7,769	**Taxable Income**	$3,759
Cash Flow Before Taxes			**Cash Flow After Taxes**
Net Operating Income	$11,757	Cash Flow Before Taxes	$9,165
- Debt Service	$2,591	Tax Bracket %	27.00% / $1,015
- Addiitons	$0	Cash Flow Per Month	$679
Cash Flow Before Taxes	$9,165	Cash Flow After Taxes	$8,150
Investment Highlights			
Price Per Sq. Ft	$31	LTV	24.00%
Price Per Unit	$33,333	Break Even Ratio (BER)	26.52%
Capitalization Rate	11.76%	Cash on Cash Return	9.17%
Debt Coverage Ratio	4.54	Rent/Value	1.78%

Meeting John the Realtor

Before I get into the numbers, a quick warning: Numbers and analysis are great and necessary, but any property can look exceptional on paper and be totally different in real life. The first property I ever analyzed was a sure thing, I thought.

The rent it could garner was good, the price was right, and the expenses and management would be perfect for my first rental. I had been looking around for a bit when I decided to call one of the local listing real estate agents. I gave him my spiel, the short of which was that I wanted to be a real estate investor, and I was interested in this one particular house. His name was John. He said, "Okay, Sonny. Why don't you come into the office, and we can sit down and talk about what you want to do?" I went.

John asked me a few questions, and probably judging by my age and the way I poorly answered those questions, he then began to explain to me that there were a few things I should consider when buying rental houses. He asked if I was going to flip the house. This meant I would make an offer, close, improve it, and then try to sell it for a profit. I said that sounded great, but that wasn't what I was after. I wanted this house to be the first of many I would eventually own.

I found a little house I liked and wanted to discuss it. I walked into the real estate office to talk about it with the listing agent. It turned out the agent had been conducting real estate business in the local market for thirty years. This man showed me all sorts of spreadsheets and calculations having to do with rental property. I'd been learning, but there was a lot here to absorb. After he brought me through a crash course on appreciation, depreciation, cash flow, after-repair value, and buy-and-hold strategies, he told me the house I was interested in was under contract already. I wondered why he walked me through and got this far if the deal I was after was no longer available. Then he told me something I later found out to be a best practice, but not true. He said I would need to save up at least $20,000 more than I had just to get started. Really? I was a bit overwhelmed, but as soon as I saw the numbers side of the business, I was hooked.

Oh, and that deal I thought was going to be my first killer buy ... With John's help, we investigated it a little further. He showed me a public resource to leverage in which you could overlay specific demographic and geographic criteria on top of the address you were interested in. It turns out that perfect rental I found was a literal stone's throw from the river that swallowed it up—twice—in the previous five years. Once

I factored in the flood insurance cost and risk, using the basic math John showed me, the deal was ... shall we say ... sunk.

I spent the next day building a quick but effective real estate rental property calculator. You saw it a couple pages ago. Basically, I found some online pictures and reverse-engineered my own. After I had my calculator set up and I knew what I was looking for, I started analyzing deals. Lots of them. Like hundreds. Right away and continuously for weeks.

After my analysis left me more comfortable with the deals I was considering, duplexes and triplexes seemed to have the best cash-on-cash ratios, so I stuck with them. A subsequent challenge was "analysis paralysis." We can get stuck running the numbers all the time and never get out from behind the desk. It's a real thing. Don't let yourself get stuck here. Develop a strategy and decide on the types of properties you want to invest in. Start getting into the doors of places that are interesting to you. Even if you still don't know how to pay for said properties, know that there are ways. At first, at least I knew there were ways... seemingly mysterious, secret ways, that only rich people knew about... but I was determined. It didn't hold me up, so don't let it hold you up. Get a feel for your market. I did this, and you know what it felt like? Well, it wasn't good.

I would not have chosen to live in any of the houses I saw during that first group of showings. Mostly, the properties reminded me of where I lived in my college fraternity days in a house with a two-inch-deep perpetual puddle on the kitchen floor. I wasn't impressed, but I knew I was at the juncture of an important strategic decision. Was I able to stomach the market I thought I wanted to get into?

BRRRR

I knew that real estate could generate longer-term wealth if I were to buy the property, improve it, rent it, then refinance it using a bank. This is commonly referred to as the BRRRR process, which stands for Buy, Renovate, Rent, Refinance,

Repeat. If this sounds enticing, it should. It's an excellent wealth-building tool and works in concert with many other methods used to invest in real estate.

Back to my realtor friend, John. He pulled up a tool on a Google Sheet that day. He called it Annual Property Operating Data (APOD). It's just an Excel or Google Sheet with some formulas built in, mostly simple algebra. I had been working with Excel as an analytics manager for years, so it was straightforward. In fact, it was way too simple—so what I'll share with you today are the calculations I built into my own tool after a few years of investing.

I always tell people who want to be real estate investors that they should begin analyzing deals on paper. Punch in the details on a calculator to find out if the deal makes sense. Learn how to "buy it right." My practice is to forecast very conservatively, but you may also be aggressive. As risky or risk averse as you want to be, you can outline worst-case scenarios that can occur with rental situations. Buying them right goes the farthest to ensure the success of the asset. To that end, I built my rental calculator tool to help me see what the "right" number would be.

Rental Terms and Metrics

There are some basic components you'll need to leverage this analysis tool to its greatest advantage. Purchase Price, Rent, and Expenses are the main throughputs, and while they'll get you most of the way there, you'll eventually want to understand all of these metrics.

- *Gross Income:* Rent, or total money collected. This is the monthly rent collected from all units in the building multiplied by twelve months. You can also include any additional income like laundry, parking or miscellaneous fees.
- *Vacancy Rate:* The percentage of time your property will be vacant. This number is usually immediately

subtracted from your rental income. I am conservative and use one-twelfth, or 8.33 percent, which amounts to one month vacant per year. Living in what's characterized as a very legally tenant-friendly state, I also keep this number high to mitigate the risk of nonpayment or evictions. Generally, though, I see 4 percent–6 percent used most often. Depending on the number of units in the building you're analyzing, you may want to go higher for a single-family and lower for a multifamily, as the number of units can be a large variable in the overall vacancy of an asset.

- *Operating Expenses:* These are expenses such as taxes, insurance, management, repairs, maintenance, utilities, and landscaping/snow removal. Other expenses can include professional services, advertising, supplies, legal fees, bank fees, and marketing. These are the costs you will pay to run the property.
- *Net Operating Income (NOI):* Gross Income minus Expenses. Not counting debt service, this is the amount of money you should expect to make per year. Income – Vacancy – Expenses = NOI
- *Debt Service:* This is the cost of any money you are borrowing. If you have a $100,000 loan at 5 percent over thirty years, you will pay $537 per month to the bank. At the beginning of your loan, about 80 percent of that payment, $417, is going toward interest.
  - *A note on debt service:* In my analysis, I do not split out principal and interest when considering debt service amounts, though you could do that if you wanted to. If so, you would count the interest payment only, like debt service, and because the principal is actually paying down the amount of money you owe, you could also decrement that from the loan amount calculation. I find little

value in doing this at the beginning of an investment, but I like to look at it toward the end of one. It gives me a better perspective of what I have in the deal, totally, as an investment sunsets.
- *Cash Flow:* (NOI – Debt Service) The amount of money you will make after you pay your debts but before you pay taxes. Cash in hand on a monthly and annual basis.
- *Cash on Cash Return (COC):* This is Cash Flow / Purchase Cash. It's the amount of cash you receive before taxes, divided by the amount of cash you laid out on the purchase, representing how much of your investment you're receiving back per year. I look for a COC of over 10%.
- *Capitalization Rate:* This is NOI / Purchase Price and is a representation of the larger investment viability. I think of this as my initial rate of return and use it for purchase analysis. Anything higher than 8% is pretty good these days, but as always, whether the Cap Rate works for you will depend on the market and the work you need to do to raise your NOI.
- *After Repair Value (ARV):* The ARV is the expected value of the property after the repairs are complete. When buying rentals, savvy investors are looking for deep discounts. When purchasing houses at deep discounts, investors need to rehab property, which can incur significant costs. For example, if an investor purchases a house for $25,000 in a neighborhood where similar houses sell for $125,000, they may be able to spend $50,000 in rehab costs for a total investment of $75,000. This amounts to instant equity. ARV is used to determine the resale value of a property or the amount of money that can be taken out of the equity later when refinancing.
- *Equity:* (Property Value – Debt) / Property Value. This is the amount of ownership you actually have in the

investment, the percentage of the asset you actually own. The main factors here are the value of the property and the amount of debt you have in the deal. Zero debt = 100% equity. Equity is the amount you can borrow against when refinancing.
- *The 2 Percent Rule:* The calculation for this one is Rent / (Purchase Price + Rehab cost). If the number is greater than 2 percent, it is considered a good deal. The value and interpretation of this metric can vary wildly among investors. While some investors are OK with 1%, others look for 3%. I am more conservative and try to get good deals on the purchase, so I lean toward 2%–3%.
- *BRRRR:* This term is defined as Buy, Rehab, Rent, Refi, Repeat. The model is sound but also relies on a number of factors to make it dependable. Basically, you purchase a property and renovate it, then rent it, which raises its value. Then you go to the bank and get a loan against the new appraisal amount, of which you try and pull out the amount of money you put into the deal. Leveraging the debt allows you to repeat the process.

Here is an example of the numbers in a simple and ideal scenario:

Purchase Price	$50,000	
Rehab Cost	$25,000	
All In	**$75,000**	
Annual Rent	$12,000	
Expenses	($2,000)	
NOI	**$10,000**	
Cap Rate	13%	($10k / $75k)
Appraised Value	$100,000	
Loan @ 80% LTV	$80,000	

Now that you know what all the terms mean and you have a basis for REI calculations, what will you do? Pick a template, get out there, and start analyzing tons of deals!

A word of caution: Know your numbers, but don't get lost in them. At first, you won't be able to *feel* if the deal is right. This will come much later. Experienced investors barely need to use a calculator like this, but using it often and using it correctly when you are new will serve you in the long run.

CHAPTER 9

Finding Money

Whether you have your own money, need to borrow it, or are planning on using other people's, one thing is for sure. You will need to have access to money to become a successful real estate investor. Many newcomers are intrigued when they hear things like, "you don't need to have money to start investing in real estate." It's true, you don't. You can definitely launch a wholesaling venture on only a shoestring budget and sweat equity. You can find people who will sell real estate and hold mortgages with zero dollars down. But if you want to own real estate, you will need to control money. It doesn't have to be yours, and it can be borrowed. There are countless ways to do this, so let's look at the most common ways investors gain access to money.

Cash

If you came into some money or have savings, as they say, "Cash is King." There are some very obvious upsides to buying real estate with cash. Cash offers are more likely to be accepted by sellers. If sellers don't have to worry about your qualifying for a mortgage, they will almost always accept a cash offer if all other things are equal. Another advantage of cash buying is time. Cash is fast. Banks, lenders, and underwriters all take time. Finally, as a buyer, owning debt-free real estate is true wealth. Unleveraged property is true ownership.

It seems intuitive and simple to purchase real estate with cash, but there are also some significant downsides. This will almost always depend on your larger strategies and plans. If you are trying to grow your real estate business, it will pay to leverage debt to expand your ability to purchase more properties. Providing they cash flow, you would use something like the BRRRR process to broaden your portfolio. We'll circle back to BRRRR in the coming chapters but the thing to realize is that if you buy only in cash, you limit yourself only to property you can afford in cash. For example, if you have $100,000, you can buy one house for $100,000. Alternatively, if you use debt leverage and other people's money, for $100,000 you can put 20% down on each and buy five!

Conventional Mortgages

There are many types of mortgages but when we speak about conventional mortgages, a few key characteristics come to mind. Traditionally speaking, a borrower first goes to a bank or fills out an online mortgage application. Banks will require that you have a percentage of the purchase price for a down payment. The average is 20% but can range up or down depending on your credit rating, your debt-to-income ratio (DTI) and your relationship with the lender. They'll run your credit, help you understand what things need to be changed for successful underwriting and then discuss terms. These include things like the amortization or time frame the loan will span, the interest rate and the repayment term. The bank uses the property as collateral and secures its debt with the property. You pay the loan back with interest over time.

Private Mortgages

Unlike conventional mortgages, where funds are borrowed from a bank, private mortgages are borrowed from an individual or private organization. These are fantastic options for real estate investors for many reasons. Private lenders are usually people you know or who are in your network. There are usually fewer requirements and these loans have, relatively speaking, a much easier underwriting process. On the flipside, in order to compensate lenders for the risk they are taking, the interest rates are usually a lot higher than with conventional loans.

Seller Financing

These are the same as private mortgages, only the lender is the person or organization you are purchasing the property from. Seller Financing or Owner Financing is where you agree to purchase a property and the owner "takes back" a mortgage. Essentially, you pay them whatever the agreed upon price is, and they allow you to borrow the remainder – or the entire purchase price – directly from them. Some of the best real estate deals I've seen have owner financing involved. If done successfully these can be highly beneficial to both buyers and sellers.

Home Equity Lending

For this bucket, I am including two specific types of money, methods I have used dozens of times. Here you have the Home Equity Loans (HELO) and Home Equity Line of Credit (HELOC). The former, HELOs are simply mortgages, often second position mortgages that conventional lenders loan to borrowers who secure the loans with their personal homes or properties. They are fixed and have the same repayment terms as mortgages.

More flexible are the latter, HELOCs. These are also usually bank loans and are very similar to HELOs or second mortgages with one variation. You can borrow against the line multiple times over the term of the loan. If you don't use it, you don't pay any interest or fees. If you borrow against it, say to buy a house or put down a payment on one, you pay the interest back according to the terms of the loan. Most often these interest rates are variable and align with whatever the market demands at the time the borrower takes the money out.

Unsecured Debt and Credit Cards

Real estate investors eventually run out of options for conventional mortgages. There are some risky ways to gain access to capital that I do not advise for brand new or inexperienced investors. If done right, borrowing unsecured debt can be extremely advantageous. It brings to mind that time I bought a house with a credit card! While I did do this, it was an auction site and it made more sense to use plastic.

The method I devised was based on borrowing money from credit card companies in the form of balance transfers. At one point, I had over 50 credit cards with more than $600k in available credit. Opening multiple credit cards with high balance limits is the first step. Then, as time passes, you continually request balance increases to the lines. You use and then pay back the lines of credit as they expire. If you have good credit, this is a step you should consider. After you generate enough credit using this method, it's not uncharacteristic to receive balance transfer offers in the neighborhood of $20k each, with 0%-3% interest over periods ranging from 9 to 18 months. I will share more about the details of the system I developed in the supplementals.

Partnerships

If you don't have money, but can provide something else,

say sweat equity or property management, you can leverage your abilities to partner with other investors who are lacking that which you have. For an out-of-town investor, an excellent way to ensure their investments are being protected is to partner with a local investor. For the out of towner, knowing their property is in the hands of someone with "skin in the game" is an assurance that they will oversee the asset as their own, because it *is* their own. In turn for providing property management, maintenance or renovations, a partner with limited access to capital may be able to provide services other investors may be looking for. Real estate is a great vehicle for problem solving and from a partnership perspective, it can be mutually beneficial.

Retirement Funds

Many of us have 401(k) plans, IRAs and other money in places like the stock market or bonds. Conventional wisdom tells us that we should keep adding money to these places for "someday." Retirement planning and saving is certainly a part of my investment portfolio, but in the past, it was the *only* part. To make sure I could make my money work best for me, I found that I could divert some of my retirement savings into real estate. Self-Directed IRAs and Solo 401(k)s are methods by which you can control the funds in the accounts umbrellaed by retirement and tax protections, if you are careful. Alternatively, you may decide that some of those funds, even at a 35% hit for withdrawing before eligible, could be used over time to make much more money than they could with the basic returns you see in the retirement funds. Liquidating retirement money should not be taken lightly. As with anything I write, I'd suggest you bounce that off a trusted professional before taking any action.

In summary, there are more ways of finding money than my publisher has ink for. The best advice I can offer here is to explore the avenues that could work for you based on the type of investing you're doing and the relationships you can build. As

I've mentioned before, the relationships you can build with real estate investors will be a strong measure of your success. You can go at it alone or you can partner with people who you can help and who can, in turn, help you. At different stages of your journey, you may find doors opening you never knew were there.

Handling your business will involve a level of risk you may not be comfortable with. I urge you to test those boundaries. Don't be reckless and always have a pivot plan, but also remember, like Bill Napier said regarding the decision to go for the touchdown rather than settle for the field goal in the 2021 Florida v. Louisiana Football game: "Scared money don't make money!" Somebody is going to have to take risks if you expect to get results. Measure them, understand them, and take them!

CHAPTER 10

Wholesaling & Off-Market Deals

Wholesaling in real estate is the act of executing a real estate purchase contract and then selling that contract to an investor who, in turn, purchases the property. It's basically an agreement to buy a property that can be conveyed from the wholesaler to a third party, the actual buyer. The front end of the process involves advertising, marketing, and market research. The wholesaler markets the fact that they buy houses and, by focusing on specific criteria, they aim to pair deals in contract with cash buyers. Wholesale deals can be done on listed real estate, but most occur off-market, with properties that are not listed on the Multiple Listing Services (MLS).

The thing about wholesaling that makes it so attractive to beginners is that it requires little-to-no-money to start. You can also make a substantial amount of money on single deals. The part many new investors fail to see is that it takes a weighty skill set to do this well. The best wholesalers have a deep knowledge of real estate markets and a transparent process for making deals. Ninety-nine percent of the time, when I get calls from wholesalers, their numbers are totally and laughably wrong.

I basically stumbled into everything I'd ever done in real estate, so I never get mad at a new wholesaler. It doesn't take much to gain a cursory amount of information about the various types of real estate investment that are available to beginners, and for me, they all fall into the natural order of things. I wanted to invest in real estate because I knew it was good for generating wealth and creating income streams, and eventually, my hope would be that it could provide me with the security I felt I was lacking by relying on my 9-5 job as the only means to support my family. Buy-and-hold was a strategy I fell into through renting my first house when my family got larger and needed more space. I paid too much for it, couldn't sell it for what I thought it was worth, so I rented it. After a couple of years, I realized I could sell it and buy two rental houses; thus, my buy-and-hold strategy grew. On the way to that evolution, I learned about a few other real estate investment methods that would support my main buy-and-hold strategy. One of the first was wholesaling.

After I had determined that buy-and-hold rentals were something I could manage and started generating income, I wanted more. I will go into it in more detail later but suffice it to say that my personal experience and mentality, while not unique, are far from relaxed or patient. When I find something that excites me and I can see how it can benefit my life, I tend to think that doing it ten times harder or faster will make everything ten times better. This isn't true, but it's how I approached my real estate career. It's also how I approached everything in my life that I consider myself to be very good at.

When it came to finding deals, I wanted to be better, faster, and smarter than all the competition. I wasn't—but I tried. I still do. I wanted a lot of deals crossing my desk, and I heard through Bigger Pockets podcasts and books that wholesaling was a way to get there. Mind you, I never intended to be a wholesaler. I just wanted to create deal flow, and that effort turned into something else. You see, the first part of real estate investing—whether you are a flipper, a wholesaler, or a buy-and-hold investor—is exactly the same. I was all three of those, and each strategy starts in the same place: finding the deals.

The term "wholesaling" can be deceiving as it relates to real estate. When you think of buying something at wholesale prices, the first thing that comes to mind is Walmart. Walmart and other large companies like it leverage their buying power to present a wholesale price value to their customers—a price only available to large retailers. The term "wholesale" makes you think of large quantities. In real estate, while there are definitely wholesaling companies and large buyers that move hundreds of properties per year, that's not a requirement to do a single wholesale deal. As a beginner, wholesaling is a low-risk, high-reward method to learn how to analyze lots of deals and establish a basis for the rest of your real estate business.

Finding Deals (Reprise)

Step one in wholesaling, as in any type of real estate investment, is identifying your target markets to find deals. You can't sell a deal you don't have, and in order to get deals in contract, wholesalers must know where to look. The best place to start is any market where you have knowledge. Personal connections in a target market always provide a competitive advantage to wholesalers. This doesn't mean only geographically speaking. Market knowledge of investor propensities, construction trends, and real estate values are all part of this, but the main point is that the successful wholesaler is looking for a leg up on the other investors in the market doing the same thing. Any connection to a market that gives a wholesaler more information that they can use to determine property values, investor preferences, and repair costs will make them more competitive and credible in the space.

Generating Leads

Once an investor has identified a market, they will start canvassing for leads. Lead generation is more of an art than a science but works best when aimed at the correct segment of sellers while not excluding potential sellers who may be on the fringe of the target market. My primary targets during the early years were single-family homes. I used a common formula that I thought would appeal to the real estate investment strategies I wanted to support. I started with the end in mind. By identifying single-family homes, my goal was to buy houses at a discount that I could either flip or hold for long-term rentals. I was interested in both opportunities, and the method I used was driving for deals and sending yellow letters.

I would drive around and look for rundown houses in nice neighborhoods. With a little research, I could find either the individual who owned the home or a group of likely people who could be the owners. Searching local real property websites, tax rolls, and internet searches were my main approaches. Sometimes I'd ask the neighbors or check the stack of old mail on the stoop. Other times, I had to get more creative and track down family members, but the result was the same.

Driving for deals can be productive because of its pinpointed nature, but the time and labor intensity make this strategy more of an ancillary or accompanying strategy for lead generation. Direct marketing, such as yellow letters, postcards, and internet marketing, are better ways to generate the volume of leads needed to ensure higher deal flow. Delivering direct mail or targeted marketing will usually involve a third party that can first generate lists of property owners who meet the criteria the wholesaler has determined will result in good leads. It may take a few tries or several tweaks to the criteria, depending on many factors, including market, potential investors, and experience.

What you want to look for are the factors that could influence an owner's decision to sell their property. Some of these factors are very obvious and are the ones to start with. A seller's age, whether they live at the property, and whether they own the property free and clear are three of the biggest factors that can influence whether they may be motivated to sell. In today's world, there are many organizations that put these types of lists together for purchase. The most competitive list generation companies have access to data tools that allow investors to refine their searches and identify a multitude of other factors as well.

Off-Market Deals and Analysis

The idea behind a lead generation strategy is to identify sellers before they put properties on the open market. Once everyone else has their eyes on it, or realtors are involved, I'm out. Most real estate investors do not want to compete with a lot of other buyers, for obvious reasons. Primarily, the demand of the open market on the limited supply of motivated sellers causes prices to rise. The fewer people who know about a distressed property, the better. You're looking for off-market deals. Off-market deals give the wholesaler the opportunity to quickly solve several problems. A solution for a property owner who has been saddled with a distressed property or who simply doesn't have the time is what they're after.

Wholesalers' attractiveness to sellers comes from their ability to close deals with cash buyers who can move quickly. Buyers who leverage wholesalers are getting discounted properties with few hassles or barriers to entry. In return for their fast cash and discounted price, buyers face the risk of missing issues that might be found through a more in-depth, drawn-out purchase process. For example, off-market deals usually do not undergo lengthy inspections or include many contingencies. They are usually cash deals, so they aren't subject to scrutiny by banks or third parties. This is the old-school, Wild West real estate.

Once an investor has found a deal, the next step is to establish its after-repair value (ARV). This will allow the wholesaler/investor to pair the property with another investor and eventually assign the contract to a motivated discount buyer. Investors want to see low prices with high ARVs. This is not a simple task and takes time to perfect. It's also the reason there are so many bad wholesalers out there. If the wholesaler can establish a good process using excellent market and property analysis, they will be able to provide investors with good opportunities.

The better the opportunity created by the low contract price and high ARV, the more the wholesaler can determine the assignment fee. Here's another place where wholesalers often make mistakes. A deal with a massive assignment fee is fine for many investors but can be off-putting to others. It's totally discretionary, but it all goes back to the deal. If the contract price plus the assignment fee is still very attractive to investors, it should not matter how high the fee is. Again, it's subjective in terms of how investors feel about it, but objective in that the assignment fee cannot make the deal too thin or too risky. With good analysis, a reasonable assignment fee, and a willing investor, the assignment of contract is a simple legal procedure that will result in each party getting what they want. The seller's problem with a distressed property is solved, the wholesaler collects the assignment fee, and the investor closes the deal.

Because wholesaling has a limited barrier to entry, with both low cost and low risk, there are lots of beginners in this space. There are also lots of bad wholesalers. Personally, I can't stand most of them, and I don't give them the time of day. The biggest reward I've experienced with the wholesalers I have encountered has been teaching them things about the markets I'm familiar with. My thought is that by sharing knowledge with them, in the hope that they will someday become valued partners or simply get better at what they do, I am giving back and supporting up-and-coming investors.

A common mistake wholesalers make when estimating a deal is poorly identifying the submarket and the neighborhood. Just going to Zillow, Trulia or Google can be a pitfall when trying to assess a property's after-repair value. Knowledge of markets and submarkets comes with time and experience, and in the absence of those, they either shoot from the hip or use a local consultant. A real estate agent who understands the market can be helpful, but they always want a piece of the pie. This makes wholesalers hesitant to deal with them. Alternatively, a local real estate investor can be a wholesaler's best resource if they take the time to develop those types of relationships—a feat they seemingly never put the requisite amount of time and effort into. Understanding local markets avoids a lot of wasted time and effort on everyone's part, so if you encounter a wholesaler who is willing to learn, bend their ear for a minute. It may pay off a great deal.

Another annoying thing wholesalers do is overreach. If the process of marketing a deal in-contract begins with poor knowledge of the local market, its already bad positioning can be compounded by greed. When wholesalers begin, they are inevitably enamored with the amount of money they can make on a single deal. My experience is that instead of making $5,000 per deal and doing a whole bunch of them, some wholesalers reach for the $30,000 deal and end up doing far fewer—or no deals at all. I get it: work smarter, not harder. No matter what anyone says, if it's a good deal, after the contract fee is added, so be it. However, greed in the form of giant markups is a turnoff.

The most important part of wholesaling is developing an accurate After Repair Value (ARV). This results from understanding markets at the local level, which can be challenging in both large and small markets. This becomes increasingly difficult when the wholesaler is not local because taking neighborhoods into account is one of the most overlooked errors.

One of the most integral parts of the finding deals and wholesaling has to do with determining renovation costs on projects. Wholesalers struggle with this because the costs vary so widely from market to market. In a market, it's certainly possible to receive estimates from two similar contractors that result in 100 percent different costs. Many of the wholesalers that call me do not live anywhere near here, and while they could take the time and do the research to gather great data, most times, they don't. As a buyer of wholesale contracts, you have to do the math and the research yourself. Oftentimes, when the wholesaler expects a large payoff for selling the contract, buyers are turned off because of their lack of effort.

The same thing about meeting investors when marketing and writing letters also holds true about wholesaling deals. If you start to advertise that you have a deal in contract and you're willing to sell the contract, naturally the group of people that are going to respond will be investors. You can test your analytical skills and calculators by bouncing these deals off those investors, and ultimately, you may develop new relationships.

As a professional wholesaler, the best thing you can do is expand your knowledge of the markets you're serving. Leveraging existing information from those already in the market—investors—is the best way to do that. Developing these relationships pays off, as it will expand the degree to which you, as the wholesaler, can become an expert in the marketplace, establishing your credibility. Most wholesalers are very low in the credibility department. In my experience, there are ancillary benefits to building relationships with investors through wholesaling.

In 2017, I was running a yellow letter campaign and found a single-family house locally. The owner was one of three brothers who owned the house. It was in a bad part of town, but the house itself was in fair shape, with paying tenants and sound mechanicals. The owners had done a good job of maintaining the property, but they were clearly just tired of being landlords. As they approached retirement age, they simply wanted someone else to take on the issues they were having with tenants, phone calls, and maintenance requests. I liked the sound of that.

I made them an offer that was entirely too low, and after a bit of back and forth, they accepted. With the deal in contract, I posted a line on my social media pages and started getting a few calls. One investor was very interested and agreed to pay me

$3,000 on top of the contract price to sell him the house. He had never seen it and asked me to provide him with the details. I asked my attorney to set up the assignment of contract, and we closed on the property a month or two later—a cash deal. I was transparent, honest, and made a few thousand bucks. The buyer became a friend and recognized that I could be an asset to him locally.

Since that first deal, we eventually went on to own over 150 units together. As a wholesaler, whether in support of a buy-and-hold strategy or not, if you follow some of the suggestions made here, you will begin to develop a deal flow. This is where the would-be flipper or buy-and-hold manager can capitalize on wholesaling. If you send out enough letters, create leads and capture enough web traffic to your "we buy houses" site, or even if you drive for deals, your pipeline will be flowing with people who want to sell you, their houses. If that excellent problem happens to you, you may not want or be able to handle all the deals yourself. These are the moments when you can still get these deals in contract and then wholesale them to your investor colleagues in the network you've been growing. I became a wholesaler by accident. I had too many deals in the pipeline and not enough money, willingness or wherewithal to buy them all. So, I tacked on a few thousand bucks and sold the contracts. Voila! Instant wholesaler.

Many investors I know have decided that they'd rather not be buy-and-hold investors. I get it. Buy-and-hold investment and hands-on management, specifically, are not for everyone, and definitely not for the faint of heart. It took great pains for me to make the decision to become a buy-and-hold investor, and if you find that you're just so much better at finding deals and leveraging marketing tools, there can be a ton of opportunities here. Personally, I like finding the deal, but I never liked giving them (or selling them) away. I'm also less convinced that this avenue is actually real estate investment.

To me, wholesaling, like house flipping, is more of a job. If you stop doing it, the money stops too. Like any business, though, wholesaling businesses can generate tremendous wealth with proper delegations, great systems, scalable models. It's a path that many take, especially if they find they're much better suited for the deal-making siding of the business as opposed to the property management side.

Wholesaling takes work and patience. In order to make it a full-time wealth generator, you would need many deals in the pipeline at one time. In order to support a staff or a team, you would have to be closing many deals per month. To get to that point, your network must be broad, so oftentimes, wholesalers need to expand beyond just one county or region. This is why I decided to use wholesaling as an ancillary part of my business as opposed to the main strategy.

CHAPTER 11

Partnerships

"Hey Dave, what's the only ship that always sinks? ...A Partner-ship!

This is what I heard when I asked John, the Realtor, about partnerships. I hoped that he was wrong. We all form various alliances throughout our lives. From the moment we are born, we need others to take care of us. First, as dependents and children, we experience strong emotional attachments to our parents or caretakers. Then, as students in school, even in our earliest classes, we were asked to pair up with other students to try to accomplish a goal. We tend to think of these collaborations as projects, not always primarily based on emotions or dependency, as we did when we were babies. We seek deeper companionship from others. Friends, significant others, and spouses are all forms of very common partnerships that most people have a basic understanding of. Sports teams, recreation, and leisure activities all involve levels of partnerships with other humans.

We typically enter into most partnerships through

informal, unwritten agreements. They're sometimes formed in ways as simple as non-verbal cues, practices, or simply, circumstances. Sometimes we make pacts. Many of these arrangements have rules, but they are often unwritten. Most partnerships we enter are fleeting, but some last forever. Examples in my life include the excellent friendships I maintain with the six guys I was closest to in high school. Another common example is marriage. I have been married for twenty years. I'd call it successful...(most days).

Partnerships in business are similar to other partnerships, and many can be just as organic and informal. This may often feel like the right way to proceed because it seems easy, having fewer strings attached, and can also feel freer. This warrants caution. Business agreements and partnerships can be highly rewarding emotionally, but may not be in your best interests all the time.

So why consider entering a business partnership? Well, why do we do it in other areas of our lives? Maybe we want something someone else has, or perhaps they want something from us. Possibly, we share common goals. Cooperation, shared purposes, and balance related to compensation—both monetary and in strengths and weaknesses—are usually reasons we choose partnerships. Ideally, in terms of goals, we seek out partners who share our objectives. Partners should agree to collaborate to achieve common objectives. In marriage, each partner typically seeks personal companionship, as well as physical, emotional, and intellectual attraction. Love. I am married to my best friend. Do you need to love your business partner? No, of course not. You can, but it isn't required. Whatever the desired outcome, you'll want to weigh the pros and cons of entering into a business partnership. One of the first questions you might ask yourself is, "Can you achieve the same results alone in the same amount of time?"

There was a moment in my life when I watched NASCAR. If I'm honest, I just like the idea of day drinking on Sundays. I was never really into it, but I did come away with one nugget that never left me. In math class, I used to hear things like "the whole is greater than the sum of its parts." It didn't seem to make sense. I thought two and two were four. However, what I learned from watching NASCAR was something different: a phenomenon called drafting. When two cars, which could separately only move at a set rate of speed, say 150 mph, drove really close to each other, one behind the other, something happened that made them go faster than either could go alone. From an aerodynamic perspective, this makes sense because the lead car faces the resistance of the air, and the trailing car, facing less resistance, moves more quickly. Both cars form an air pocket, and their individual strength comes together to produce faster speeds. In other words, they absorb the resistance and capitalize on it in a way that benefits both. Partnerships aren't always equal shares. In this example, the lead car absorbs more resistance and has to work harder, while the trail car experiences the internal benefit, which results in pushing the lead car faster. When considering how partnership looks relative to the other race cars though, they move faster than any of the rest of the competition could alone.

Most people don't achieve anything worthwhile on their own. Partners in business likely bring different things to the table. When a partnership is running on all cylinders, beautiful things can happen. One partner complements the other, and a kind of symbiosis can occur. The main characteristic they exhibit, which sets them apart from the competition, is that each partner's strengths and weaknesses are complemented and counterbalanced by the others. Perhaps one partner has the money, while the other has the sweat equity. One partner may have relationships and expansive networks, while the other is willing to run the back office operations. It is 100% worth analyzing each partner and identifying their prospective contributions before entering into agreements. Failure to complete due diligence can very easily and very quickly lead you into regret, trouble, and debt.

Advantages of Partnerships

When I started doing real estate deals, I initially resisted forming partnerships. I still do. I am a selfish person, and if I need to rely on someone, I like when the only person to lean on is me. Call it self-centered, yeah, it is, but I don't really see it exclusively that way. If I am the one calling the shots, then I am the only one accountable. I do not like putting others at risk. If I am the one screwing up, then it is at my own peril, not yours. Those are seemingly safe bets, but they have significant downsides too.

Without partners, I would never have been able to expand my business in the way I did. I couldn't have gotten into bigger deals as quickly, and I would have missed out on learning the things my partners had to offer. That's a huge potential miss. Everyone, no matter how smart or how accomplished, has something to offer, something you can learn from.

It turns out that having smart people around to bounce ideas off is a huge advantage. Partnerships based on trust still involve risk. How will you know if you can trust someone until you do it? It's more like faith in that way. But hedge your faith. Make sure you do your homework before deciding whether someone else either has what you want or can offer you a complimentary business proposition.

A clear and concise operating agreement (OA) is crucial to a partnership. The record of the agreement, the percentages of ownership and the responsibilities and rules must be outlined in order to allow for smooth sailing with partnerships. Business partnerships can go wonderfully, and while there are very long and complex books on how to navigate them, I learned that the most important parts of forming partnerships and writing operating agreements boils down to three simple items:

Roles

What is each partner responsible for doing? Knowing and specifying each member's responsibilities is possibly the most important facet of the partnership. This can be tricky because you don't always know what the partnership will look like down the road. Still, you want to map these out as accurately as possible. Try not to overcommit and ensure you overdeliver. If you are making commitments, especially those tied to time frames—such as forever or in perpetuity—you want to be very sure you can keep your commitments, and that your partners are accountable for maintaining theirs.

Decisions

How are partnership decisions made? If there are two partners and they each have an equal say, what determines the tiebreaker? If there are three partners and each partner owns different shares of the deal, how are decisions made? Are some decisions based on %, and others unanimous? It will pay to understand this decision tree in very granular detail. The value of having a clear understanding among all members regarding who decides the direction of the partnership and how those decisions are made cannot be overstated. The last thing you want, especially when business is not going great, is confusion.

Exit Strategy

How do partners exit the relationship? Your exit strategy may not seem necessary as the excitement of starting the business is flowing, but do not skip outlining this step. Once you are in, you want to know the ways out. Trust me, this is a significant development. Life will happen, and if something goes wrong with one of the partners, you will want to be very clear on how to get them out and/or how to get yourself out. Without carefully considering your exit strategy and the exit strategies of your partners, you may end up stuck without a viable way out, other than through legal proceedings. From experience, those are not fun.

    Approaching the first partnership I entered, the other two guys knew each other beforehand. That made me comfortable in some regards, but also led me to negotiate for unanimity in certain aspects of the partnership's decision-making. It never mattered, because these guys are just amazing people, but it could have. You never know.

CHAPTER 12

Flipping Houses

Out of all the real estate investment methods, this is often the one considered the "sexiest." The idea of paying something like 50 percent of the retail price for a house, putting 20 percent of its eventual value into the rehab, and pocketing the other 30 percent is my kind of math! Many people will disagree with me, but the finished product versus the "before" pictures is just as gratifying as the dollars in the bank. Maybe it's short-term gratification, but the finished product, when done correctly, makes all the pain, time, and effort totally worth it.

The concept is simple, but the pitfalls and opportunities for failure are extensive. To succeed as a house flipper, you first need to understand the highest price you can afford to pay for a property. This requires a solid understanding of the maximum renovation costs, which in turn depend on your familiarity with market conditions, contractor price ranges, and time frames. Achieving this level of insight typically requires either years of experience or conversations with many knowledgeable people. Start with education, take some action, and then build your experience.

Without experience, education is an excellent substitute. Like many others, I enjoyed house-flipping shows. They were dramatic, enticing, and they made flipping houses look easy and glamorous. In real life, it's not easy or anything like those shows.

By the time I was writing yellow letters and putting out large swaths of "We Buy Houses"–style marketing, I had a few deals under my belt. My thought was that while I was optimizing the property management side of the rental business, I needed a flip project running simultaneously. The flips would supply the cash I needed to further the buy-and-hold strategy. They also kept things super interesting for me. I learned a lot about contractors, pricing, and presentation from flipping houses. It presented itself as a great alternative when the deal seemed right.

I encountered three kinds of deals when I was marketing. If it was an affordable buy and could be brought back to life and rented using basic renovation tactics like painting, replacing fixtures, and cleaning, I'd consider it a buy-and-hold deal and try to add it to the portfolio. If not, I'd consider it a wholesale deal unless it met a few other criteria. If it were in a good neighborhood and I could get it cheap enough, it would start to make sense to transform those deals into homes, ones that first-time home buyers would want.

These are the types of homes people would see as the finished product on those house-flipping shows. During the 2010s, these shows were ubiquitous, and all first-time homebuyers were watching them.

Once a deal was in either the buy-and-hold or the flip bucket, there were more details to iron out and verify. A big factor to consider when deciding whether to flip quickly or hold has to do with taxes. Short-term sales involve higher income tax payments. Another consideration is the extent of the renovation or the time it might take. For example, if you are flipping, you really want the renovation to be complete within three to six months. If it's on the shorter side, your hold time, including the time it takes to sell and close, becomes more important. If you sell short-term, you are going to pay higher taxes. If the renovation takes a longer period of time, you may want to consider the deal a delayed flip. A delayed flip is when you hold a property for more than a year, take more time on the renovations, in order to avoid short term tax payments. If your holding cost is low, or you've leveraged the deal at a really great interest rate, maybe you're not worried as much about the hold time.

An additional consideration related to the hold period has to do with the market you're in. If you happen to be in a rapidly appreciating market, your returns may allow you to forego tax considerations to strike while the iron is hot. These decisions should always come down to your return on investment (ROI). If it costs you more to hold the property and sell it after a year than it does to renovate it quickly and sell it short-term, paying higher taxes, you have your answer. The way sold assets are taxed on a short-term basis vs. how they are taxed after holding them for a year can really make a huge difference to your bottom line.

The most mainstream calculation used to determine the viability of a flip deal is the 70 percent rule. Like other investment methods, house flipping involves finding good deals, usually on distressed properties. Buyers use wholesalers, real estate agents, foreclosures, auctions, and other means to get their hands on houses that have an After Repair Value (ARV) that is 30 percent higher than it will cost them to buy, hold, finance, renovate, and sell. The 70 percent rule states that if the purchase price, plus holding cost, plus rehab cost equals 70 percent of the ARV, then you are golden. Anything less can still be a good deal but is riskier. The following table represents an example of a deal that meets the 70 percent rule:

70% Rule: Purch Price + Rehab <= 70% of ARV.	
Purchase Price	$40,000
Rehab Cost	$30,000
Purch + Rehab/Hold	<=$70,000
After Repair Value	>= $100,000
Meets 70% Rule	$70.00 / $100,000 = 70%

Not all deals are incredible flips, and not all flips should be done as fast as they can be renovated. Delayed flips can also be a great way to create some short-term capital while you rent a home. They can also be used to avoid paying large income tax sums on financial assets that are bought and sold within a year. In other words, you'd prefer to pay the minimum 20 percent capital gains tax on profit made from an asset held and sold after one year, as opposed to paying the short-term, less-than-one-year-held taxes you would be stuck with if you bought and sold the asset within a year. The short-term sales tax is calculated at your income tax bracket level, which is probably higher than 20 percent. There are other good reasons not to sell short-term. Let's look at a real-world example.

Delayed Flip Case Study

I found a two-bedroom house that was mid-construction. We'll call in Bear Ct. This purchase was handled by a real estate agent and known as a pocket listing. If you can develop relationships with local real estate professionals, you may start to have them give you a preferred status, and they will run these so-called pocket listings past you before they put them out on the Multiple Listing Service (MLS). What this really means is that you will have the first crack at deals before the rest of the world. The realtor may only have a few preferred buyers, but sometimes they have a lot. Their goal is to close a strong deal quickly.

Developing relationships with realtors almost always relies on honesty and transparency. Real estate professionals know that there is a lot of competition out there among other agents for your business, so they don't want to have their time wasted by tire kickers and people who aim to use their expertise without reciprocating. Ultimately, it's a competition for loyalty, but as I've said to many realtors over the years, loyalty is a two-way street. Most realtors pretend to be loyal; others walk the walk. In the long run, it matters little how they conduct themselves. What matters most is that you keep your side of the street clean of treachery and dishonesty. Approaching things with cards on the table, facts and data always trump opinions. Try to keep it as real as possible. This could mean telling realtors that you are going to use the people who fit best with your business. You don't get a lifetime loyalty card from me unless we've done a lot of business, and our trust is established.

Bear Ct was one of those listings a local agent kept off the MLS until he showed it to me. I received a call from a real estate agent, and he told me to meet him at the address in ten minutes. Still working my day job, not everyone realized I just couldn't drop everything for real estate. I liked it that way. I met the realtor at the house in ten minutes.

Not only was the seller there, but there were also a few other local investors already there poking around. The seller was mid-renovation, and for whatever reason, they were not going to be able to finish. Now they were looking for a quick cash sale and a way out. As I passed one of the tired old landlords, he commented, "That's way too much work for such a small house." I liked the sound of that.

Whenever someone said, "Way too much work," my ears perked up. One of the greatest things about being driven (and borderline insane) is that I would jump at challenges to crush people's expectations of what acceptable levels of work are. I don't judge them, but I know that, "way too much work" is not a thing in my life. It never was.

I entered the house and saw that everything was basically torn up. No kitchen, no floors, and so many new and unused materials. I had to take a video to make sure the inventory was accounted for later when I closed the deal. If I was going to make an offer, I had to make sure I got whatever I could.

It was clear to me that the guy trying to flip this house had no idea what he was doing. It's not a bad thing to walk into, though many contractors don't like it. When you follow someone else into a half-done (or 25 percent done) job, you need a talent for correcting mistakes. Fortunately, by this time in my investment career, I was no longer doing the work myself. I had a contractor who would complain about it, but who could definitely correct the mistakes this seller was making right before my eyes.

I tried to get as much information about the job as I could. It may not be important in the short or long run, but I still wanted to know as much as possible. I found out that there was a marital dispute leading up to this sale. It seemed like the guy working on the house may have been building it to escape his wife. I felt bad for him, as I usually do for people who are selling their property under duress.

In the end I knew two things. One, he needed the cash I had to offer and he needed it quickly. Anything to get him out of the predicament he was in was going to make him happy. Two, even though it was only a two-bedroom house and wouldn't be easy to sell, I knew I could fix it up nicely. It had oak floors under the carpet (almost the first thing I look for), and the bones and corners told me the house was very solid and mostly square. I ran the numbers. It met the 70% rule with room to spare. I knew I could flip it for a significant profit. I went for it, and he accepted my ridiculously low, cash offer.

There are a lot of details and more time than you think that go into each decision along the way to a successful house flip. In this case, the decisions on what to renovate and what will pass for a great sale can be subjective. I almost always do the same basic things, but each one is its own animal. For this one, I refinished the hardwood floor. There is never a time when I would forego the opportunity to refinish hardwood floors in a flip house. To me, you simply don't put vinyl of any kind over the top of oak. It's a travesty, and I see people do it all the time. It's in every model for every flip I've ever done: if hardwood floors, then refinish them. There's also something about the smell of polyurethane. It smells like a new house.

I also always install stainless appliances and a tile backsplash. If you see a tiled kitchen floor, a tiled backsplash, and stainless appliances, you may be distracted enough not to notice that I spend less time and effort on cabinetry. If I were living in the house, I'd always replace the cabinetry, but I find that new home buyers are often much more interested in the new floors and high-end appliances than the type of wood the cabinets are made of. I used middle-of-the-road cabinetry, fixed and repaired all the damage in the walls and sheetrock, and painted the whole place. We always paint everything. We rehung the old doors, replaced the hardware, and replaced all of the light and plumbing fixtures.

A lot of times, one of the criteria for flips versus rentals is square footage. While larger houses are more appealing to buyers, smaller ones are cheaper to flip. This was a very small house, and with the renovations kept to a small footprint, in just a couple of months, I was ready to sell it. I was thrilled at how fast the renovation went, and the money I spent on it was less than I originally thought. Everything went perfectly leading up to the point where we brought in the cleaners and staged it with small-sized furniture. Then I put it on the market.

Crickets. When we put it on the market, nothing. No calls, no questions, no chatter, nothing. Maybe it was bad timing, a market lull, or just a two-bedroom house that wasn't functional or competitive for the first-time home buyers I was aiming for. The house was gleaming, with lots of newness. I decided after a few months and a price drop that I would have to rent it to avoid any additional loss caused by a house sitting idle. In the state I was investing in, there were very high property taxes, and the carrying costs of a perfectly good house sitting there did not justify not renting it. I waited and waited until I could wait no longer.

Eventually, I put it on the rental market, and of course, my listings exploded. While there were not a lot of people looking to buy a two-bedroom house, there were plenty looking to rent one. I had people out the door wanting to rent this place. I received top dollar rent from a highly qualified tenant. After his first year, he renewed for another. Once the tenant left, I decided to take another shot at selling it. This time, the market was higher, and I decided that while the house could continue to be a great rental, it didn't quite fit in with my portfolio. I decided to cash out and sell it. Here's a look at the math on the Bear Ct delayed flip. Let's look at the comparison between renting it before selling:

Purchase Price	$42,000
Reno Price	$38,000
All-In Price	$80,000
Sale Price	$125,000
Profit	$45,000
Tax Owed < 1 Yr	$14,850
Tax Owed >= 1 Yr	$9,000
Tax Savings	**$5,850**

Had I sold the house one year before, I would have been taxed at the regular income tax rate of 33 percent. Because I waited for longer than a year, I sold the house at the capital gains tax rate of 20 percent.

By holding onto the house, not counting the $12,000 or so made in rental income profit, there is a savings of $5,850 by selling it more than 365 days after I bought it. In addition, the sale price we got after the year was higher than it might have been in the previous year for two reasons. First, the market appreciated, and home values went up. Second, I would have been more inclined to sell it at a discount in the short term because I received no offers.

It's a testament to the buy-and-hold proposition to create wealth, for sure. Not everyone wants to hang on to assets for 366 days. I get that. Holding and carrying costs can also be a big factor, but if you map out the basics and predefine your worst-case scenarios, you will, more often than not, benefit most from the hold part of the buy-and-hold deal. Not the sexiest part, but I guess…to each their own. For me, I knew flips were fun, delayed flips were a way to save tax dollars, but buy and hold was where it's at!

CHAPTER 13

Vacation Rentals

Getting started in real estate looks different for everyone. When I started, I wanted to grow my portfolio rapidly and would do anything I could to acquire more units. I still feel that way, though diversification has also sparked my interest. Many of my rentals are nice, and I would live in them. Others I would have lived in years ago, but my standards have changed. As I get older, my creature comforts are not extravagant, but my requirements are different from those of my twenties. This seems to match what I've seen in the market as well—older renters and higher earners are looking for a better class of products. In the vacation or short-term rental space, depending on supply and demand, you can charge more for a higher-quality product, so meeting market expectations is especially important.

My management team asks this question when we are working on, managing, and showing our units: "Would you live there?" If my team says no, we start asking more questions and defining the controllable and uncontrollable factors in their answer. My portfolio initially did not include vacation rentals, but it does contain some short-term rentals. But let's face it, everybody needs a vacation sometimes.

As a mainly buy-and-hold landlord, renting from other

people is fine, but only if I must. My family and I went on one, maybe two, vacations a year. As the kids grew, we traveled a little more with sports and visiting family members. Each time we traveled, I'd think, "I have a lot of houses in my hometown. What if I had some in towns I'd like to vacation to?"

Before COVID, we visited a Central American country. Aside from a cruise, it had been my first time outside the United States. We ate fresh fruit, enjoyed drinks on the beach, and took in a bit of a wonderful culture with a rich history. I do this everywhere I go on vacation, but as I sat on that beach looking at the palm tree-lined coastline and the dense jungle beyond it, something ignited. My perspective and worldview expanded.

There were definitely people there with the same mindset as mine, but I think most people toy with things like this. I don't. If something seems like a cool idea, and the factors that could make or break that idea seem reasonable, I go for it. As I sat on the beach, I declared, "I'm going to buy a house here someday." And you may remember how I feel about "someday." I had a belief, made a decision, and started taking action.

In my local market, we've used Airbnb selectively, especially in student areas. When a furnished house was available for a few months or longer, listing it on Airbnb boosted profitability. Listing for longer periods seems to turn a short-term rental from occasional weekends to a fully booked calendar. Short-term rentals are a mature subset of buy-and-hold strategies, though managing them well can be challenging for traditional property managers.

Furnishing student rentals and managing a strict leasing calendar are one thing, but going from a bed, dresser, and desk to a hotel-room-like setup involves significantly more work, time, and attention—especially to get it going. There are so many details you wouldn't normally consider, but are required if you want to attract guests and have them rate you well. Sheets, pillows, soap, utensils, small appliances, bathroom items, Wi-Fi, and dozens of other details make short-term renting its very own niche. You can make the transition if short-term rentals are available in your market, but it's better to start with that end in mind than to pivot to it just to try and make a few extra bucks.

Here are the goals I set for our first vacation rental:

- *One-Month Trip.* The plan was for my family to spend a month in Central America, visiting various places and experiencing life there on a longer-term basis. We were trying to determine where we might like to stay on our larger, longer, subsequent trip, and if we were to buy a house, where that would be. The first trip would be designed to help us find a place in the country that supports our needs as a family and where we could contribute to society. Wherever we ended up, it simply had to *feel* right to us.
- *Learn and Speak Spanish.* Another goal was for the whole family to become fluent. My wife was a Spanish teacher, which gave us a huge advantage, but we'd not yet been successful in forcing ourselves to use the language at home. Well, there's no better way to learn a language than through immersion, and that's what we needed. We knew becoming fluent wouldn't happen in a month, but we needed to start somewhere.
- *Find Investment Property.* As an investor, the idea of renting or staying in hotels was antithetical to my DNA. On our month-long trip, we met with real estate agents, investors, and managers as we began plans for the next trip! The longer-term goal was to own a vacation rental property in Central America, with the investment covering our lodging expenses during our stays.

I first had the chance to visit Central America several times. My wife had been there previously with students on a summer language trip and had been raving about it ever since. We flew in, rented a car, and drove pretty much across one of its countries. We are a family of five, and, while we don't do it very gracefully, we're fairly used to traveling. Our three boys were nine, seven, and six years old at the time. We were looking for a home away from home.

Most of the people were courteous and kind, the climate was hot and humid, and the waves and beaches were spectacular. When we ventured away from the beaches into the jungles, we felt like we were in a movie. In fact, many movies, including *Jurassic Park*, were filmed in Central America —and it's easy to see why. The plants are larger than life, the landscape is stunning, and the wildlife is far more intriguing than anything we'd seen in a zoo. It felt like traveling back in time to prehistoric days.

For our first jaunt to Central America, we divided our weeklong trip into two segments. We spent the first few days on the Pacific coast near the town of Playa Carillo at a beachside resort. For about a hundred dollars a day, we got a hotel-sized room with two queen beds and a patio. The resorts all had pools. We received a sit-down, hot breakfast every day, and we ate our lunches on the beach at a table the staff brought down for us. We drank from coconuts straight off the trees, sliced open by the local machete-wielding vendors. The hotel staff shuttled us back and forth to the beach whenever we wanted to go. It was relaxing and wonderful.

The wildlife was unlike anything we'd experienced. One night, our kids were playing on a small playground at the resort. My middle son fell off the swing onto the ground, which was a very normal thing for him. When he got up, there were some pretty sizable ants crawling all over him. He hates bugs! If you do too, let me tell you, it will probably get worse before it gets better —but it will get better. After a while here, you'll start to become more accustomed to all the wildlife, including the bugs. It's not quite like a journey under the *Temple of Doom*, but the bugs in that movie are real, and they do live in the jungle. On subsequent trips, we began to feel numb to it—not always, but mostly.

By the end of our few days there, we had seen all

the animals we'd put on our shortlist, including an extremely active juvenile sloth. We were hooked, but admittedly, we'd experienced it in a pretty pampered way. We'd be looking for something different on a longer trip next time.

As soon as we got home, we started planning the next trip. Could we somehow make a month-long trip work? How could we afford it? What would happen to our friends, our house, our business? Could we really all start speaking Spanish? What about money? Other people were finding and buying investment properties and making this a lifestyle. I knew we could figure it out, too.

If we could stay in a place we owned—a vacation rental that eventually paid for itself—I'd be thrilled. Do we have some lofty goals? Sure, maybe. But in my forties, these upstate New York winters were really killing me!

In September 2023, we bought our first vacation rental—a three-bedroom, two-bathroom house in a small South Pacific town. And so, the journey continues.

We pulled the kids out of school and traveled to our house in Costa Rica. People thought we were nuts. I thought we were a little nuts, too, but I tell everyone the same thing: Most people spend their lives wondering what might have happened if they had followed their dreams—what they could've done or who they should've been. I don't want to be one of those people who wonders why they didn't do things. I want to be able to tell you how to do it, what made it great, and show you that you can do it too!

Here's the secret: It's an inside job. It's all in our heads. We are the only ones holding ourselves back. You can do huge, crazy, massive things. You can reach your goals and set them insanely high. You just have to be willing to take the risks and ignore the fears that push you to take the easy way—especially when people in your life tell you that you can't. I'm not saying you have to ditch those people, but if you want to, you might reach the highest heights. They want you to fail because it makes them feel better about their own insecurities. Be immune to that. Don't judge, but don't listen either. The only person who can make you fail is you. Own that.

CHAPTER 14

Buy and Hold Rentals

Find deals, make offers, buy them, renovate them, and rent them out. Leverage them with debt if you want to scale. Simply stated, buy-and-hold rentals are the best way I've found to create, maintain, and build wealth. Combine the income with the tax advantages, the ability to leverage your investments, and appreciation (the icing on the cake), and you have a tried-and-true option for establishing your empire. Create systems where these little energy mills chug along collecting rent, and you'll be able to generate long-term wealth and profitability.

Compared to house flipping, which can generate lots of taxable cash, this niche focuses on building a lifelong income stream and wealth-generating business model. Let's look at a few types of buy-and-hold strategies that I know will work for you because they've worked for me.

Market Rate Rentals

Market rate rentals are simply rentals where the open market determines the rent. My entire real estate portfolio was built on market-rate, buy-and-hold rentals. While there are many subsets and types of rentals within the buy-and-hold segment, market rate is how most rentals are classified. Basic supply and demand dictate what landlords can charge for these units. They are generally simple, basic houses or small apartment buildings with one to four units and one to three bedrooms in each.

These rentals are found throughout every region of the country and are mostly owned by regular people like you and me. Most small businesses in the United States are small landlords.

The tenants for these properties are typically working-class or middle-class individuals, though they can vary widely in economic status. Each region's rental market has its own characteristics, and neighborhoods everywhere have unique dynamics based on zoning and local laws. However, one thing remains constant: property owners invest in rentals to meet housing demand, charge a premium, and, if they run their businesses wisely, generate cash flow over time.

There are usually few or manageable restrictions at the neighborhood level on who you can rent to and where you can apply this age-old strategy. In my case, I focused on five or six local municipalities, with an emphasis on two-to-four-unit buildings. I centered my marketing on these types of units, and when I found them, my strategy was to hold them forever—or at least for five years.

This five-year timeframe wasn't based on anything more scientific than the sense that it gave the property enough time to justify the work required: finding the deal, financing it, fixing it up, and starting to generate income. Of course, I ran the numbers every time—dozens of times—but after a while, "back-of-the-napkin" math was enough to know if it would be a good investment. This is the advantage of experience. Having done this so many times, I could easily spot pitfalls and avoid costly mistakes. Eventually, this became second nature, a stark contrast to my earlier "fake it till you make it" approach.

Scaling Up to Multifamily

Eventually, one-to-four-unit buildings started to feel a little boring. I'm a problem—I always seem to be looking for what's next, the bigger, better, shinier thing. Being satisfied is not something I'm good at. Especially in real estate, I've always been enticed by what's next.

As my portfolio of residential units and buildings grew, I became increasingly interested in larger buildings. The economics made sense, and I used to describe the jump to the next level this way: "Just add another zero." That's how I approached it.

The steps involved in analyzing a four-unit building are the same as those for a twelve-unit building. Sure, the boilers are bigger, the square footage is larger, and there are more tenants, but the multiples and the potential profits are far more exciting at a larger scale.

After just two years as a real estate investor, I partnered with a few people and bought my first twelve-unit building.

From an economic standpoint, market-rate buy-and-hold rentals—and all buy-and-hold rentals—must meet specific criteria to accomplish the goal of creating wealth. At first, I focused on small residential units and used the 2 percent rule to determine whether the deal made sense. Once you establish what the base rent should be, you can calculate how much you can pay for a property.

The 2 percent rule states that, for an investment to be worthwhile, the rent should be 2 percent of the property's value or purchase price. For example, in my early years, I targeted houses in the $50,000 range and aimed to rent them for $1,000 per month. While these numbers shift as property values increase, the benchmark goal remains the same. However, the rental market and the owner market don't always align.

In markets with higher property values, rental income often falls into the 1 percent range. This is normal and acceptable as long as the property cash flows. A market-rate buy-and-hold rental property must cash flow—the higher the percentage, the better. This isn't rocket science, but sometimes getting there can feel like taking a trip to the moon.

Student Rentals

There are many submarkets within the buy-and-hold arena, and when I started my business, I explored a few of them. Locally, I knew there were several colleges, and I decided to try tapping into the student rental market. However, students in my area lived in a very small zone, making deals hard to find. It also seemed like investors already in the market had a tight grip on it.

The market was tricky. Investors knew that student rentals were more profitable than standard market-rate rentals, which drove property values higher in the areas where students lived. Still, if you could find a deal, the margins on student rentals were significantly better. To capture those margins, however, the properties had to be treated very differently than market-rate rentals.

Because the town I primarily invest in is a college town, the specialized student rental market soon became a sizeable portion of my business. While most of my portfolio consisted of standard rentals, the student market was enticing and required an understanding of subtle and critical differences.

Student rentals are great, but they come with unique challenges both before and after purchase. One major factor is the seasonality of the market. Student rental markets vary widely, and no one-size-fits-all approach exists. In my area, timing is crucial because the leasing cycle is tied to the academic calendar. Missing key windows can leave you with fewer and less desirable options.

For example, in September and October, right after the college semester begins, the market is flooded with groups of students searching for housing for the following June. The leasing season runs from June through May, which creates a timing challenge. If you're in the middle of purchasing or renovating a student rental and the property isn't ready to show by September or October, you'll miss out on most of the best tenants.

When this happened to me, I sometimes took the opportunity to renovate the properties further. Other times, the houses simply sat vacant until the next opportunity to rent came around in January. During January, you could target inbound transfer students or kids moving out of other places mid-semester. While transfer students were great, students moving mid-semester often brought higher risks.

With such a specific and small market contingent, if you miss both the September–October and January windows, you might need to consider renting to market-rate individuals. These are regular tenants willing to rent a furnished room in a shared house with others. You can probably imagine the risks that come with that arrangement.

The student contingent works well when all tenants share the same mindset. Higher education is their focus, and they generally stick to routines—going to class, sports practice, the gym, and meals together. However, broadening the tenant base to include unrelated adults often creates chaos. Differences in mental health, habits, schedules, and lifestyles can turn a shared house into a breeding ground for problems when the tenants lack the familial bond that makes such living arrangements work.

As with any submarket, understanding its nuances is crucial to gaining a competitive advantage. Failing to grasp these subtleties can lead to significant pitfalls and wasted time. Longtime student landlords know their clientele well. They've dealt with the specific challenges of renting to students and have learned how to address them.

I've seen many small landlords try to break into the student rental market without being prepared. They think, "I'll buy an old house, fix it up, and rent it to students for twice the price." What they don't see are the hidden costs that can cause their investments to fail. For example, students may only be permitted to live in certain areas. Trends in the student marketplace can be hard to track unless you're closely connected to their social circles. If the market expects utilities included in the rent and you're not offering that, your property may sit vacant. New landlords can succeed in the student rental market, but only if they do their homework.

Commercial Rentals

While I primarily focus on residential properties, owning and managing commercial real estate can be a great investment strategy, albeit with its own set of risks and rewards. On a small scale, commercial rentals can be managed similarly to residential rentals. The owner collects rent from businesses leasing their space, but beyond that, there are many differences.

One advantage of commercial rentals is longer-term tenants. Businesses often sign multi-year leases, leading to more stability. Additionally, commercial tenants often pay for custom buildouts, which can increase the property's value. For example, during one of our projects, we considered converting a former library into a rentable space for a nonprofit organization. We weren't willing to cover the upfront costs for the buildout, but the tenant had secured grant money to customize the space to their needs. This win-win scenario highlights how owners can capitalize on tenant-driven customizations.

Another major distinction between residential and commercial rentals is lease structure. Commercial leases often include triple-net agreements, where the tenant pays for rent, utilities, taxes, and insurance. Residential leases rarely include these terms, however, commercial properties come with drawbacks, such as prolonged vacancies and economic downturns that can affect a business's ability to pay rent. If the business fails, you lose the tenant and may face eviction proceedings.

Choosing Your Market

Whether you pursue a niche submarket or stick to the standard market-rate industry, there are countless avenues to success. Conducting market research and performing a thorough analysis of high-level trends is an excellent starting point. Building relationships with people familiar with your target market is equally important. Partnering with experienced investors can also be a smart way to enter the field. If you have capital and they have experience, a partnership can bridge the gap.

Ultimately, what will make or break your success in buy-and-hold real estate investing is property management. Even if you buy the right property at the right price and secure great tenants, poor property management will eventually lead to failure. In my small market, I've seen many New York City investors come in thinking they can dominate the local scene. They're attracted to the lower property values, minimal barriers to entry, and relatively high rents. But they often lose their shirts by relying on bad realtors, bad contractors, and bad property managers. Property management is the number one key to succeeding in market-rate rentals.

CHAPTER 15

Property Management

As you already know, there are lots of ways to invest in real estate. With this book's main focus being on buy-and-hold rentals, many of the practices that support and maintain that style of investment hold true across other types of investing too. For example, when your goal is flipping houses, you still want to get the best deal you can, but your main focus will be the 70 percent rule as opposed to the 2 percent rule or cap rate. Finding deals and buying them right is investment-type agnostic.

But what if your goal is not single-family rentals? Maybe you are interested in multifamily units or apartment complexes? Things that will differ slightly are the ways you pursue these deals, the means by which you manage the investments, and how you finance the deals. While similar in their foundations, the tactics you employ could be very different. This section is devoted to helping you establish your management criteria, independent of what stage in your investing career you are currently in.

To Self-Manage or Not to Self-Manage

Any way you look at rental property, it must be managed.

Find the deal, buy it right, fix it up, get good tenants—but no matter what you do, if it's not managed, it will fail. Every rental property requires management, but how you plan to handle that management can significantly shape your purchase decisions. However, it's important not to let concerns about management unnecessarily limit your investment choices.

Self-management can be great, especially if you are just starting out. On the flip side, it can also hinder your ability to scale. If possible, I would recommend it, because it is the quickest, most surefire means to learn the business. Furthermore, while you do not need to self-manage, if you are able to at some degree, it will pay off because you are going to have to manage your property manager. Doing it yourself, even for the short term, will help you (1) establish the true value of a great property manager and (2) allow you to define what great property management is for your business.

Self-Management — Brooklyn Anthony

There was a pattern I noticed: remote owners with large portfolios in the towns I was investing often had properties in poor condition. Meanwhile, local landlords with smaller portfolios seemed to have well-maintained properties. These landlords weren't part-time investors—they were fully hands-on, driving plows, mowing lawns, and collecting rent themselves.

I remember one yellow-letter campaign I did where a local owner called me. He asked me over to his house to discuss what I was doing. As an older investor—and I found this a lot following yellow-letter campaigns—he was generally interested in how I was doing things and, I think, wanted to see if I was the real deal. I still had very little money at the time, but I was all piss and vinegar. Laser focused on growth and huge management. Thinking back to that version of myself, I am envious. I had an intensity that people could see. It was coming out of my pores.

After accepting Anthony's invitation to meet, I entered his

modest home, and he began sharing a bit about himself.

Anthony was a proud Brooklyn native who had worked a manual labor job in the city before retiring to an upstate town to pursue his dream of buying, renovating, and renting houses. His approach was what I'd call traditional: he started with a lot of cash, relied on realtors to find deals, made solid cash offers, and hired contractors to handle renovations. Once the homes were fixed up—matching the quality of the one he lived in—he rented them out. He used yard signs to attract tenants, waited for calls, and carefully screened applicants.

From our conversation, I estimated he owned about ten properties, ranging from one to four units each. With some quick math, I figured his portfolio was worth about a million dollars. For a new investor like me with no money, it was incredible to sit across from a retired city worker who had become a multi-millionaire. Millionaires don't always look how you expect them to. Anthony said it took him about ten years to build his portfolio—too slow for my ambitions—but seeing his success in person left a lasting impression.

He asked me plenty of questions and eventually shifted into sales mode, given that the meeting was sparked by a letter I'd sent about buying one of his properties. In the end, I got more value from our conversation than I ever could have from purchasing his properties. Anthony was far too experienced to sell at a discount, which is what I had hoped for. We briefly discussed the possibility of his owner-financing the property, but without a relationship in place, he wasn't interested.

The meeting with Anthony—and others from my yellow letter campaigns—offered countless lessons. Even if I hadn't landed a single deal, the knowledge and community connections were worth the investment. I was so engrossed in the business that I was eating, drinking, and dreaming about it. Obsessed.

Takeaways from My Meeting with Brooklyn

Anthony

- What Millionaires Look Like - Millionaires come in all shapes and sizes. Meeting Anthony showed me that a real estate investor could look like a garbage man—and that was fine by me. Anthony's humility stood out. He drove an older car and focused on building lasting wealth through real estate, not on flashy displays of success. That's exactly what I wanted: real estate, security, and lasting wealth. The way this particular millionaire carried himself drew me in and surprised me. He was a real millionaire next door.
- Work Ethic - Anthony's work ethic set him apart from others who had tried and failed at doing what he did. While talent and charisma are valuable, I've got unique respect for people who commit to relentless hard work. Anthony embodied that. He cared deeply about his tenants and dedicated himself to every aspect of his business, from managing contractors to addressing tenant issues. I saw in him a quality I wanted for myself: pride in where he came from and how he got to where he was.
- The Maintenance Bear - Anthony handled every aspect of property management himself, from collecting rent to cutting grass and plowing snow. Before showing me his garage, he said, "To be a great landlord, you need to dig your tenants out of the snow so they can get to work and be able to pay the rent. Don't give them excuses." Inside was a plow truck and snowblower, tools he used to ensure his tenants could always get to their jobs. I wondered if I'd ever be able to afford a plow truck—but at that moment, I definitely couldn't.
- Scalability Challenges - Anthony managed ten properties as his full-time job, earning around $100,000–$150,000 annually while working 20–30 hours a week. It was a solid income, but it wasn't my goal. I wanted to replace

my current job's income multiple times over. I realized that while I shared Anthony's work ethic, his approach wasn't scalable for the goals I had set for myself. There are only so many hours in a day, and with a family to think about, I knew I'd eventually need help to manage properties at the scale I envisioned.

A self-manager and one-man show looked like something I could actually do, but I wasn't willing to sacrifice my family and day job to make it happen. That wouldn't make sense either fiscally or psychologically. It didn't align with my "why." I had to consider the best ways to scale my business over time and how to allocate my time efficiently toward that end. If I were doing $10-per-hour work, there was no one to do the $100-per-hour work.

Years after this meeting, I would wrestle intensely with letting go of day-to-day tasks in favor of higher-value efforts. This one thing continues to be one of my greatest struggles in business. I can do the $10-per-hour tasks better than anyone else. But should I? The answer is: Yes! This remains the perpetual plight of the "doer," and while I'm better at it now, the pattern hasn't entirely left me yet.

Overall, my meeting with Brooklyn Anthony changed the way I viewed the local self-managing investor. While Anthony was doing an excellent job and cared for his tenants like family, he was micromanaging his properties. The return on his management style was twofold.

First, with his finger on every lever in the business, he seemed to have peace of mind and consistent results. He had a close, day-to-day relationship with his tenants and was constantly on the ground, protecting his investment. Because of his hands-on approach, Anthony minimized wear and tear, deferred maintenance, and actual depreciation. As a result, his properties appreciated in value more than the average rental.

Second, Anthony had the satisfaction of knowing about every loose screw, and he kept things at a level he found personally acceptable. This gave him confidence that his investments were secure.

On the other side of things, while I knew his hands-on management style was the best, I also knew it wasn't scalable unless more people became a part of his organization. Personally, I wanted to create a business, not just be a landlord or property manager. Furthermore, Anthony's model is much tougher to navigate financially when you are leveraged with loans, as I was, and Anthony was not.

Developing Scalable Systems

At my 9-to-5 job, one of my main responsibilities was automating manual systems. For a large organization with diverse operations across multiple locations, the work and methods varied significantly from one office to another.

To develop more efficient IT systems, we often began by analyzing the manual processes each location had in place. These ranged from truck routing, to inventory audits, and tracking key performance metrics. Simplifying these complex, multilayered systems required us to start by auditing each location's procedures. From there, we identified the most time-consuming tasks and determined which ones could be automated.

This experience became invaluable when I started managing my rental properties.

Early Management Challenges

At first, my operation ran much like Brooklyn Anthony's. However, there were some key differences. My margins were thinner, I had less time, less money, and less knowledge about what worked and what didn't. While these may sound like disadvantages, they actually forced me to think critically about how I managed my business because I had to create greater efficiency to operate at a profit.

If you happen to have an abundance of any of these three

resources—time, money, or knowledge—your strategies might differ. For this section, my goal is to outline how to save time and create opportunities to conserve money and gain knowledge.

Property Management Software

One of the most frequent questions I get from new investors is about property management software. Like almost every other real estate or investing question, the answer depends on your business, your goals, and your requirements. There's no one-size-fits-all solution.

One thing is certain: if you plan to scale your business in an effectual, streamlined way, you'll need a robust property management solution. However, if you're just starting out, you don't need to spend a lot of time or money setting up a system you might not yet need. The threshold to start preparing for a comprehensive system typically comes around 15 to 20 units but if you know you are going to scale, earlier is fine. It will take some time to acclimate and leverage any system you choose.

In the meantime, you can use simpler tools, like Excel. To this day, I've found no tool more powerful or customizable than Microsoft Excel for tasks like property analysis and tracking manual data. Keeping track of rental statistics doesn't have to be as complicated as software companies suggest. The value in creating your own tools is paid off in your innate understanding of the things you are measuring.

If you're tracking your income and expenses, you have two of the main metrics needed to understand how your business is performing. If income exceeds expenses, you're making money. Cash flow is the name of the game.

Virtual Assistants

If I had to highlight the single most important factor that makes my business run so well, it would be our virtual assistant (VA). Using platforms like Fiverr, Upwork, and freelancers.com, you can delegate lower-impact, repetitive tasks almost immediately.

Virtual assistants have been game changers for real estate professionals, but as with any other aspect of business, someone must manage them. Scaling a well-oiled business machine involves delegation, freeing you to focus on the high-value, high-visibility aspects of your business. For example, my VA assists with scheduling appointments, paying bills, chasing rent, and answering maintenance calls from tenants.

That said, certain tasks still require a personal touch. I wouldn't send a VA to a Zoom meeting with a bank or investors. While virtual delegation saves time and money, mistakes in this area can be costly. Sensitive tasks or those requiring nuance may be better handled by someone closer to the ground.

I used to spend countless hours paying bills, sending rent reminder emails, setting up payment plans, and screening applications. Today, I handle none of that—it's all managed by a trusted VA. While VA services can be expensive depending on their complexity, we pay about half the U.S. minimum wage for full-time assistance. The return on investment for VA services has been tremendous.

CHAPTER 16

Delegation

I was a DIY homeowner for ten years before I became a real estate investor. During those years, I botched every type of home improvement project imaginable. I messed up plumbing, framing, sheetrock, and electrical work. I sanded asbestos, breathed it in, built a deck on top of a septic tank, and even cut off the end of one of my fingers.

Now, these don't sound like great things to be proud of—and I'm not—but they helped me. Being in a financial situation that forced me to do much of the work myself taught me that every problem has a solution that can be worked through. This logic also scales. However, believing that I had to be the solution to every problem wasn't going to allow me to scale my business and would ultimately stymie my success. I had to break through this mindset.

I remember being in the kitchen of a house on Saint Charles Street I had bought for $22,000 in central New York (not to be confused with St. Charles Place, which costs $140 at the beginning of a game of Hasbro's Monopoly, a game that always ends in a bloodbath). It was 11 p.m., I had worked all day at my job, and then gone over to the house to continue its renovation.

I had paid a contractor about $350 per window to install ten windows in the house. I still had a little money left in the budget, but I always found that I could do work on my rehabs much cheaper than I could hire it out for. As usual, I was running out of cash. I had purchased four houses over the previous six months and was starting to get in over my head.

At the time, I didn't know what I know now. While I undervalued myself and directed my efforts toward tasks that might have been better handled by someone else, I felt like I had no other options. There simply wasn't enough money, so I thought I had to do it myself.

This was my fifth rental. The year was 2017, and I was so tired and broke that I lay down on the floor, stared up at the ceiling, and just asked for help. None came. I was out of gas, out of time, and out of everything. I wanted to give up. Something had to change.

It was time to make a decision. Was all of this worth it? I couldn't see an end in sight. Sometimes, when you're at your wits' end, you can't see any other options. That's when the insidious thought of quitting creeps in. The reality was that other investors weren't lying on the floor of their rental houses at 11 p.m. on a Tuesday, exhausted and out of options. Maybe some were, but I doubted it. They didn't talk about this at the meetings I attended. Someone else must have been handling issues like this *for them,* I thought.

I had carried out the first steps of the investment process. I found the deal and bought the house "right." Now, I needed to bridge the rehab gap to get the investment cash flowing. The longer I waited, the longer it would take. But I had no more time or energy left. I decided to do the last thing I ever want to do when I can't solve a problem myself. Backed into a corner, I asked for help.

I called a friend. I was straight with him. "Eric, listen. I know you've been interested in what I've been up to with the rentals. Well, in fact, it's not going so great. I'm struggling with renovation stuff, and I simply can't afford to either stop or keep going."

Without my even having to ask, Eric said he'd be over

tomorrow. He'd bring tools and, for a modest hourly rate, help me get the work done. Why was that so difficult? Why do I always have to get to the point of total exhaustion and impending doom before I do what so many others do on a regular basis? These are questions I'll attempt to answer in another section, as they might be too personal for most readers. In a nutshell, though, it comes down to ego and pride.

No one is perfect, and my defects often show up when I start to think I'm the center of the universe instead of just a very small part of it. I was extremely fortunate to have a friend like Eric. The guy is a true family man, with a decorated and honorable military service in his background. He's one of those people you wish you could be like. With a life dedicated to helping other people. his character was something I always admired. I was thrilled to have him by my side.

Eric and I fixed that house up over the next couple of weeks. He had a day job too, so we worked when we could. I paid him cash, and he worked cheaply for the extra money, which, as it turned out, his family really needed. I had my first employee and got a glimpse of how my need for help could also solve someone else's problem. All I had to do was let my ego almost kill me before I became humble enough to ask for help. Shocking, I know.

Because I understood what was going on with the house, I could manage Eric's time alongside my own, and we got the project done relatively quickly. These projects never go as fast as I want them to, but hindsight always softens that frustration.

Some people don't have to go through this phase to pay for help or hire contractors. I want to point out that my frugality in this regard reflects only one way I've handled things. It may not be the best way. Personally, once I gained experience with projects, timing, and scope of work, I could outline and document job sheets much better. When I'm flipping a house or completing a longer-term renovation, I use a set of documents I developed specifically for those purposes. Then I leverage the preparatory work, drawings and documents, to seek out and execute plans with contractors.

Today, I don't spend any time swinging a hammer, though I'd love to. That night wasn't the last time I worked on a house, but it was the last project I did entirely by myself. My first year of taking action as a landlord and real estate investor was extremely hands-on, and that was the path I needed to take to learn that there were other ways.

As a landlord or manager, it's not a requirement to lay flooring or unclog drains, but someone has to do it. What I discovered at Saint Charles Street was that, while I saw my inability to do everything myself as a failure, asking for help actually allowed someone else to succeed in an area of their life they wanted to expand.

You see, one of the coolest parts of real estate investing is that every deal is different and requires a whole new set of problem-solving skills and criteria. After a while, especially with rehab and property management, these sets of problems start to feel more familiar and can often be solved in much the same way. Finding the right person for the job becomes an integral part of a rehab. How you go about doing that can be painful—especially if you're as stubborn as I was during the St. Charles Street job. Or you can build estimates into your budgets for contractors, employees, or friends to help you. If you do get in a pinch, or see one coming, don't be afraid to ask for help. And don't wait until you're borderline suicidal to do it.

Redefining Your WHY

Sometimes, results make you question your path. My experience at St. Charles Street forced me to reassess my pace and the risks I was taking. Personally, I have one speed and trajectory: More. While this mindset drives high impact, the life balance I hear other people talk about feels mythical to me.

When I began my path toward financial independence, I did so under extreme pressure. I never wanted to hand over my security to someone else or to a business I worked for. I approached it with a fervor that isn't perpetually sustainable without draining resources from other areas of my life. At times, I need to step back and question my motivation. Money can get in the way. Time gets in the way. My behavior gets in the way.

When I'm laser-focused on a goal, other important things can seem irrelevant. My personal journey in this regard has been long, broad, and at times traumatic. Drive is a wonderful thing, but obsession can harm the very things we're trying to protect. Throughout my real estate journey, I had a family, loved ones, a job, and other responsibilities.

What I realized after the St. Charles Street job was that I could still pursue my goals but I could also help others. By harnessing my drive and sharing it, others could benefit. In fact, that realization is the main reason I wrote this book.

Considering how our businesses and goals impact others —especially as job providers—is a great way to redefine the "why" behind your goals. Once I saw that growing my portfolio and making progress toward financial independence could help my friend Eric, it opened my mind. It allowed me to share my business and become a larger employer. It was the definition of a mutually beneficial relationship. This was the first time I redefined the "why" behind my business, but it wouldn't be the last. Over the years, as my business grew, I redefined my purpose several more times in order to compensate for changing goals.

Transition from Worker to Manager

Making the transition from hands-on doer to delegator and manager isn't easy, but it's necessary for a successful business owner. At the time, it felt incredibly difficult. Impossible, even. Having my finger on the pulse of the rehab side of the business saved me money, but it consumed my time. The cost-benefit analysis made sense at first, but if I wanted to grow from twelve units to fifty, I needed to approach things differently. Self-management and doing all the work was satisfying and necessary early on, but it wasn't scalable.

I've made this kind of transition before, with excellent results. But when you can't see the forest for the trees, you end up with a skewed perspective.

When I was twenty-four years old, I met a guy in a bar. I drank like a maniac back then, among other things, and I was jobless at the time. I had recently lost another great job due to my behavior and habits. Back then, it felt like the entire world was against me. What I didn't realize was that the world wasn't against me, I was against me.

For about a year, I wallowed in local bars, drowning my sorrows in dozens of Heinekens. I was broke and one day in the bathroom of a classy joint called the Toddler House, a friend of a friend asked me a question: "How'd you like to make $1,000 a week installing satellite dishes?"

I got his number and joined him the following Monday, traveling around the boroughs of New York. He paid me $25 a day as training pay while I learned the trade. Each morning, I'd climb into the back of his van at 7 a.m. We'd start on Long Island and head out to wherever the work was—sometimes New York, New Jersey, or Connecticut.

He taught me some terrible lessons and habits. Eventually, he taught me the job and I got the hang of what he was doing. Soon after, I started to see how shoddy his work was and realized he wasn't a very skilled craftsman. What he was, was a businessman. He was making several hundred dollars a day, while he paid me $25 to do all the work...

After some time, I got out from under him and was running my own routes. He was still getting a cut of my pay, but a lot less than before. Eventually, I was outpacing the other technicians and caught the attention of the local regional manager. He got me out from under that guy for good, and I became my own contractor.

I never had anyone working under me, but I took to the work like a man possessed. The job paid on what they called "piecework," meaning I was paid per job completed. I loved it. The faster, harder, and more efficiently I worked, the more money I could make.

First, $1,000 a week was the standard goal for six-day workweeks. But within a few months, I made $2,000 a week—and sometimes $3,000.

Eventually, my girlfriend and I decided to move to another part of the country. I made a few calls, spoke with local satellite dish installers, and had a couple of positions lined up before we even arrived. I started working for a local retailer and then for a larger contractor, handling jobs for bigger service providers.

In less than a year, I was the top installer in the region. Soon after, I was completing more work individually than anyone else in the country. I loved it. Every step was an opportunity to improve efficiency. The way I held the tools, climbed the roofs, placed the hardware, and made phone calls—it was all carefully refined to boost productivity and eliminate waste.

Eventually, I was making far more money than most people ever earned in this line of work and had developed an unmatched level of expertise. Was I perfect? No. I cut the right corners and dodged the right people to propel myself forward. It was business.

Then, something that happens to high producers happened to me. They asked me to be a manager.

My experience didn't prepare me for managing other people, and I was nervous about the prospect. I was offered the opportunity to manage an entire local office overseeing about seventy-five technicians across twenty counties and five states. I had to make a decision. No way! I didn't want to do it. This is a particularly troubling practice that happens all over the business world. My managers at the should have known that being a top producer did not automatically mean that I would be a great manager. In fact, the odds of that happening were very slim. This is the exact practice that sets so many first-time managers up for eventual failure. The good news for me was, I also didn't know this at the time so I pondered the options as best I could, only as I saw them from the perspective of a producer, not a manager.

For one thing, the money I'd make as a manager would be less than what I could earn as a worker. That just didn't sit well with me. And what about my reputation? Would my coworkers think I'd sold out? Would they respect me or get behind me? I had a lot of doubts.

After a conversation with my wife, I laid them all out on the table, pros and cons style, like this:

Pros	Cons
No more outdoor work	Might not make as much money, at first
No more work in icy winters	I might fail
Less driving	People might be mad at me
Fewer long road trips	
Less physical exertion	
Far less risk of injury	
Smoother hands	
Fewer work hours	
Manager training	
Systems training, technology	
Corporate culture	
A new business perspective	
Chance to help coworkers	
Opportunity to improve safety	
Chance to be a voice at the table	
Corporate trips	
Company vehicle	
Wearing nicer clothes	

The managerial position probably wouldn't be a sixty-hour-a-week job. But what about scalability? What about the upside potential? And what about the risks I was already facing—like falling off ladders or driving constantly? I was young, adventurous, and risky—some might even have called me insane.

Was I going to "get off the ladder," or was I going to stick it out as a laborer forever? It took me a week to decide. As you might have guessed, I took the managerial position.

You see all those pros on that list? That's great—I see them now too. But I didn't see them right away. Thanks to an intelligent, loving wife, I had someone in my corner who could.

You could argue that her fear and sense of self-preservation drove some of her input, but the key was, I listened to her, and we weighed the options together.

This is a perfect example of what partnerships hinge on: trust and respect. My wife felt strongly about this decision. While she didn't pressure me unduly, she helped me see that others were looking to me—and to us—to dig deeper and find something they already knew was there: leadership. I wasn't a manager yet, but I was already a leader. God bless her. I'm so grateful she saw that in me and I trusted her enough to believe her, even if I didn't believe in myself.

I was basically a kid when I got the chance of a lifetime. This was the most pivotal business decision I had ever faced. If I'd tried to make it alone, I would have resisted. I would have chosen the easier path. At that time, I hadn't yet learned that the path toward fear is almost always the path you're supposed to take. It's the path of courage. It's the path of success.

It was exciting too. I don't know what they saw in me back then, but the team managing those operations gave me a chance—and I almost threw it away. If I'd listened to my own fears and short-sighted vision of success, I'd have stayed in that technician position and plodded on.

Could I have been happy? Yes, of course. I probably would have been happy. But would I have unlocked new potential? No, I wouldn't have. Probably not for a long time, if ever.

CHAPTER 17

The MIB Airport Traveler

Having had that experience almost ten years before St. Charles Street, you'd think I would've realized sooner that asking for help and delegating responsibility were essential. You can look at it two ways.

In whatever I do, I try to manage systems to their full potential. If there are manual processes or tasks that can be delegated, I believe delegating too early can hurt scalability and effectiveness later.

Think of a single guy traveling for business. His preparation starts long before the trip. He gets the pets, yard, and house in order. Even for a short trip, there's a checklist: mowing the lawn, handling the mail, and setting the Nest thermostat to adjust the temperature while he's away. Some tasks may be automated, but most are manual.

In the forty-eight hours before departure, his to-do list grows. He still has to work, but now he's adding air travel prep. He pulls out his suitcase, ensures his clothes are clean and ready, and packs with precision. He knows exactly what to bring, where it goes, and how to stay within carry-on limits. If plans change, he adjusts easily—he's traveled a lot and has a system.

Twenty-four hours before the trip, he checks into his

flight, prints his boarding pass (old habits die hard), charges his devices, and gets a good night's sleep. On the day of travel, he arrives at the airport one to two hours before boarding. The process is second nature: he knows what to do at security, pulls out his laptop, takes off his belt and shoes, and places everything in the bins. He passes through, redresses, and moves on without issue.

For him, it's a well-oiled process, honed through dozens of trips. It's intuitive now, crafted through repetition. That's exactly how I used to travel when life was simple.

Now imagine that same traveler, but add three kids, a wife, multiple cars, houses, and employees. Change the carry-on bag to checked luggage and add passports for international travel. Extend the trip from a few days to months. Instead of one flight, there are three. This requires an entirely different level of coordination, preparation, and planning.

Can you picture the family at the airport? How many families are there? How many destinations? Now, expand your view to everyone else at the airport. As you approach, you notice Uber drivers, taxis, shuttle buses, and private cars. Every traveler has a unique itinerary, yet the chaos is managed. The systems governing air travel are carefully designed to maintain order.

As travelers, we learn to manage our roles within these systems. To us, the process may seem chaotic because we're not familiar with every nuance. The more we use the systems, the better we get at navigating them. A seasoned solo traveler can adapt more easily than a family traveling together for the first time. But what if that family were replaced with a group of solo travelers? Imagine a busload of Men in Black agents arriving at the airport with perfect precision—every move synchronized, every step efficient. That's how I envision my business processes.

None of those Men in Black processes could exist without extreme focus on perfecting each step first. Only then can we plan to automate. That's why I had to install floors myself for a while. That's why I avoided spending money on problems I thought I could solve for free or at a discount with DIY solutions.

It's why I ran my own projects, hired my own staff, and answered my own tenant calls.

My approach to automation and delegation has always been to solidify processes before scaling them. While this strategy has its downsides, as a new landlord and property manager willing to invest personal time, it was worth it. Today, the number one strength in my business is accountability—personal accountability.

I built the processes by doing them manually. My value proposition, or whoever builds the process in a business, is ownership. No one can follow my process and tell me that it caused a problem. Of course, exceptions arise, and they present opportunities for improvement. That's a good thing. Refining systems to withstand time, technology, and scalability is what makes them great.

Now, let's go back to the single MIB traveler. Before he gets into the van with the other perfectly efficient travelers, consider how he would react and adapt to changes. Let's say he adds a checked bag to his plan. Could he handle it by himself? Sure. Backpack on, roller board on the left, large roller suitcase on the right. A one-man show, still functioning fine.

Now, let's add another bag—maybe two more. Could he still manage on his own? Maybe, but odds are it would come at a cost. He could alter his perfect process to keep doing it himself, but as more bags (representing additional manual processes) pile up, he'd no longer be able to manage his role effectively within the larger systems he's operating in. These systems could include the airport, road rules, his family, his job, and even his psychological, mental, and physical well-being. He could sacrifice those too.

Perhaps he tries to carry all the bags anyway. He stacks two on his head, starts taking steroids to get stronger, and makes multiple trips back and forth to the airport. He knows there are better ways to handle this, but he has no time to stop and figure them out—he'd miss the plane! So, he keeps pushing, determined to do it all himself in the time he has. At first, he's even successful.

But now he looks insane. Massively strong, drenched in sweat, and sprinting through the airport regularly, people are starting to wonder what he's doing. They begin to stare at him strangely.

As he continues these frantic trips, the bags feel heavier, and their number seems endless. He can't remember it ever being this hard, but he doesn't see any way out. After a while, new problems emerge: flat tires, extra charges, missed flights, no time to recover. His suit is now in tatters. His iconic MIB glasses are broken, and he has no time to replace them. He falls repeatedly and injures his leg.

Despite all this, the bags keep piling up. He thought he was better. He thought he was smarter. Limping past airport checkpoints on crutches, he curses and yells at the people trying to help him. He wonders how he ever got into this mess.

This was me, lying on the floor at St. Charles Street.

The image of the airport traveler is obviously ridiculous. But for me, there was something oddly appealing about it. This illustration wasn't just about highlighting my own personal insanity or my attraction to chaos within order. It was to show that there are processes other people are using—processes you can adopt—that will help you scale from a small landlord to a larger one.

Whatever "larger" means for you, I don't know, but I'd suggest aiming higher than you think you should. I used to dream of 100 apartments. Then one day, I heard someone with fewer apartments than me say, "I'm aiming for 1,000 units." I thought, if he's aiming for 1,000, why am I only aiming for 100? That day, I changed my goal to 1,000. I'm not there yet, but I've far surpassed my original goal of 100.

The airport traveler thought he only needed to carry one bag, but his plans changed on the fly. If he had known from the start that he'd need to carry 100 bags, wouldn't his process have looked different? I think it would have.

The goals you've set for your business are probably too

low, but this isn't about setting higher numbers. It's about managing toward your goals efficiently. You can change the number of units you want, or you can leave it the same. What I urge you to consider is how you got here and how you're going to get there.

Every business book you'll ever read includes this quote from Sally Covey: "What got you here won't get you there." And it's true.

CHAPTER 18

Tenant Management

If you're only ever going to have one to five rental units, that's fine. Are you like Brooklyn Anthony, planning to do it all yourself? Or do you want to be like one of the MIB travelers, passing along your knowledge to the next MIB traveler and leveraging well-versed experience to ensure processes run smoothly? Whether it's five or five hundred, if the MIB traveler approach appeals to you, you may already value time and efficiency. If not, I implore you to consider it. Even if you only have one side gig, you're not looking for another time-consuming job. When the dust settles someday, no one ever looks back and says they wish they spent less time with their family and friends and more time working. Having a busload, trainload, or planeload of MIB-like travelers managing all your business processes and systems could be another way to go.

For me, I want the MIB travelers to build the planes, fly them, land them at my airports, and take the other travelers where they need to go, for as long as they need us. If you build your people and systems properly, then maybe, before you're too old, you can start doing the things you love—like surfing in Costa Rica—while your team of MIB travelers handles your luggage and ensures it all gets to the right airports, smoothly. If that's your goal, I can help you. That was my goal, and it's what I'm doing right now.

The plight of the "airport traveler" suggests that refining tasks and processes should start manually, with the goal of fine-tuning, automating, and increasing efficiency over time. What does this mean in the world of property management or real estate investing? At each step of the way, there are opportunities to improve parts of the real estate investment (REI) process. For me, it begins with marketing, advertising, and securing deals. From there, it moves through the rehab, wholesale, and renovation phases. Depending on your strategy—flip, hold, or wholesale—the paths will diverge.

If you're a buy-and-hold investor, even if you plan to hire a management company, management is where you'll make or break your success. Even the best management companies need oversight. If you choose to take your eyes off them, that's fine, but eventually, you'll pay a price for it.

Managing Residents

At the very beginning of my real estate investor journey, I have to admit, my focus was mainly on providing security and well-being for my own family. However, it didn't take long for me to realize how good it felt to provide secure, nicely renovated apartments for the people in my community.

At the time of this publication, I am self-managing 300 units. My portfolio includes single-family houses, multi-unit houses, midsize apartment buildings, and a large 44-unit apartment complex. I don't claim to know the best way to manage this portfolio, so I constantly adjust strategies, refine tactics, and seek out efficiencies and opportunities.

When it comes to managing tenants, one main thing to always keep in mind is this: tenants are people, just like you and me. They're individuals who have decided that they're going to rent an apartment in your area. The term "tenant" signifies that they've come through some advertising or marketing channel, passed your screening process, had their application approved, and signed a legal agreement with you or your company.

Generally speaking, this means you are responsible for holding up your end of the bargain, and they are responsible for holding up theirs. Simply put, they will pay the rent and not damage your property, and you will provide them with the things outlined in your agreement. For residential agreements, this typically means a warm, safe, and comfortable place to live. Putting political views and biases aside, doesn't everyone, at a basic core level, want that?

Bernie - The Tired Old Landlord

I know—and have known—dozens of landlords and thousands of tenants. People in each of those groups live every kind of way you can imagine, and you can almost never tell by looking at them how they probably live. I know landlords, millionaires even, who live in near-squalid conditions. I also know tenants on public assistance who live in pristine, sparkling apartments. They're all human beings.

Whether you're someone who treats people with respect or not, if you're going to run a business—which is what being a landlord is—you should consider how you view and treat others. As I began my real estate career, I looked to others with experience. There were parallels in my life at the time that led me to seek out examples of people I wanted to emulate. You've probably heard the saying, "If you want to be a millionaire, hang out with millionaires." While inflation may have lowered that bar, I tried to follow that advice.

In my journey, I encountered a local landlord, we'll call Bernie. Bernie was an interesting character—think of John Candy and Chris Farley as a less energetic hybrid. He was sort of unhealthy-looking, and so was his truck. He drove a pickup filled to the brim with the tools of his trade. Tenant garbage, tires, TVs, cans, grass—you name it. You could spot his truck coming because you couldn't really see him behind the wheel, only the papers piled high on the dashboard, blocking the windshield. I have no idea how he managed to drive.

I'm not trying to trash Bernie at all. He was a tremendously hard worker. I absolutely loved him. Kind to his friends, giving of his time, and helpful with his experience, he really was a great guy! He helped me in countless ways. He let me use his lease, guided me through notice and eviction processes, and gave me candid pointers about the people I'd eventually be dealing with.

When I started out, I thought I'd be so good at this that I'd never have an eviction, never get a code violation, and never have to deal with the police. I was wrong on all fronts, and Bernie knew exactly what I was in for. I remember him laughing aloud and smirking, saying, "Okay, sure, Dave…more will be revealed."

I learned so much about land lording from Bernie. He took my calls and shared his knowledge freely. I knew he owned a lot of property, most of it with 100 percent equity. No mortgages! He was even holding mortgages for others and buying and selling houses for cash. To me, he defined success. He was where I wanted to be. If you had enough money in the bank to buy a house for cash, that was "rich," to me.

But Bernie also had things I didn't think I wanted. I hate to admit this, but it's true. The biggest takeaway I remember from those early days with Bernie was how jaded he seemed. It made me reevaluate my own "why." His attitude sometimes made me question whether this path was right for me. It could have been the timing. People go through all sorts of things in their lives. I knew he was struggling with his marriage, and he was so supportive of his family that their health issues seemed to weigh on him, like John Coffey from *The Green Mile*. I worried he'd have a heart attack soon.

Bernie didn't always have great things to say about his tenants. I think the combination of family stress and tenant troubles took a toll on him physically and mentally. He was a hard worker who genuinely cared, but it seemed as though his good intentions were buried under layers of disappointment.

At the time, I had no idea what it did to a landlord when tenants didn't hold up their end of the bargain. I couldn't understand the toll it took on an owner to stand by while a tenant ran water on purpose, ripped out copper pipes, or hurt their kids inside your property. The frustration Bernie endured —what little I saw—was enough to make me look down on him unfairly. All I could see was a callous old landlord, working endless hours with no apparent satisfaction. That wasn't the landlord I wanted to become.

Moving forward, however jaded I may have been about Bernie or his life, I vowed never to forget that tenants aren't all bad. They're just people who deserve a chance. In hindsight, I've been burned badly for giving chances to people who didn't deserve them. But I've also been pleasantly surprised by people who made good on the chances they were given.

You won't find sentiments like this in most business books. They'll say, "Businesses exist to make shareholders money and minimize risks toward that end"—a lesson straight out of my Managerial Finance class. But life isn't all business when you're a housing provider. The commodity we deal in may be real property, but the essence of what we do as residential housing providers aligns with the motto of my business: *We provide great homes for responsible people.*

Ultimately, managing tenants is about managing people. People can be managed in all sorts of ways, but I always start by ensuring my side of the street is clean. If I've provided a safe, warm place to live, and my staff has treated tenants with respect, we've done our part. If not, we fix it. Of course, as in any legal arrangement or business partnership—which is what a landlord-tenant relationship essentially is—interpretations will vary, and problems may arise. Here's one example of how such interpretations can lead to issues.

Johnny Roses – The Professional Tenant

I first encountered Johnny Roses as I was reviewing applications for one of my newest acquisitions in my third year of real estate investment. For the purposes of this book, we'll call this asset the Bluebird. The Bluebird was a twelve-unit building. In my area, back in the early '30s, they built a lot of very nice six-unit buildings, three units on each side and three stories high. Later, in the '60s, as the population peaked, savvy investors and builders split these buildings down the middle, separating from front to back and creating twice as many apartments. The Bluebird is a textbook example of this. It was the second one of its kind I purchased, but not the last. I loved them because, under all the paint, grime, and abuse, they were solidly built properties. Architecturally speaking, they were designed with class in mind—hardwood floors, beautiful trim work, and, if no one put in a drop ceiling, cool ceiling designs. Unfortunately, the Bluebird had been painted at least twenty times over the years. This wasn't a huge value-add rehab purchase but it was a great deal. I had to have it!

Before my team and I ever walked into the Bluebird, we knew a few things about it. It was blue. It was vacant. The current owner owed the city tens of thousands of dollars in water bills. We surmised that a pipe froze, and water ran for a long time without being detected. This has happened to me before. It sucks. Anyway, the owner wasn't giving it away, but he was definitely selling at a discount. Holding on to a vacant but freshly painted building was going to be painful, but I thought we'd be able to get it up and running a few units at a time. It needed fairly easy renovations and lots of appliances. It had sat unattended for long enough that the scrappers started pilfering the stoves and refrigerators, which was totally fine by me. I figured we'd have it at least somewhat up and running in a couple of months. There was one thing, though. A lot of people were coughing and starting to call off sick. Did I mention that we started work on the project in February of 2020?

COVID was raging by the time we started getting apartments rented. It wasn't as crazy as it would eventually get, and we just figured it would end soon, so we began renting apartments. In fact, we actually relaxed our requirements in order to provide more low-income housing. I remember getting the call from Johnny Roses. I was in my office in the basement of my house as I explained to him that, because he lied on his application, we were going to have to reject him for a rental in the Bluebird, or anywhere else for that matter. I wish the call had ended there, but it didn't.

Johnny pleaded with me to listen and hear him out. After a few minutes, he came clean. Well, clean-er, let's say. He explained that he was actually sleeping on the floor of a friend's apartment and had no choice but to leave that fact undisclosed because he feared he'd be rejected for not having a strong rental history. I explained to Johnny that we have strict rental policies that were based on business decisions we had made. In fact, I made them based on my understanding of housing law, the business partnership I was in, and finally, from common sense.

The problem is, I'm a softy, and I really try to see the best in people. I figured if I gave Johnny a chance – a chance he and I both knew he didn't really deserve - maybe that would go toward ensuring that he did his part at being a good tenant. I also hadn't been put through the COVID wringer yet. This was soon made possible by COVID and local government insanity. I'll go into that hell later.

I told Johnny I would talk to his employer and call his personal references, which I did. They all spoke highly of him, and I could verify he had money, employment, and what seemed like a reasonable basis for fudging a fact on his application. For some reason, I put myself in his position and asked myself if what he did was deserving of continuing to sleep on someone's floor when I had a perfectly good apartment that he could afford and no other approved tenant. Bottom line—I knew the risk, and I took it. The stress of what was happening in the world impacted my decision, but alas, I made it. And then I paid for it... for the next three years.

The first thing to consider when you are screening tenants in your area is the law. My properties are situated in two states, New York and Pennsylvania. In one of those states, there are many more laws to consider than in the other. If you are making decisions on where to invest—not just in the town where you live, like me—then you had better get well-versed on the local laws regarding fair housing.

The June 2019 Tenant Protection Act

The Tenant Protection Act, signed into law by Governor Andrew Cuomo in June 2019, aimed to tackle New York's housing crisis and give tenants stronger protections. It added new rules for landlords, expanded rent regulations, and tried to stop practices like harassment and rent gouging. While it sounded great on paper, the reality for landlords wasn't so simple.

Highlights of the Law

- Rent Regulations - Rent control expanded to cover more apartments, and landlords faced limits on how much they could raise rents, especially after tenants moved out.
- Evictions and Legal Help - Tenants got more time to respond to eviction notices and the right to legal representation in housing court.
- Harassment Protections - A new state office was created to handle complaints about tenant harassment, with tough penalties for landlords found guilty.
- Education and Oversight - Landlords now had to inform tenants of their rights, and a Tenant Protection Unit was set up to oversee enforcement and educate renters.
- Rent Overcharges and Gouging - Tenants had up

to six years to report illegal rent increases, and landlords found guilty faced fines and had to pay back rent.

There were mixed reactions but tenant advocates loved it, saying it gave renters the tools to stand up to bad landlords. Landlords, on the other hand, argued it made renting out properties riskier and discouraged investment in housing. The law's goal was to balance power between landlords and tenants, but whether it did that—or just made life harder for landlords—is up for debate.

The Cost of a Professional Tenant

Following the onset of COVID and the subsequent eviction moratoriums, tenants who stopped paying rent at the Bluebird were protected. They didn't have to pay rent, while we had no choice but to continue paying taxes, water, heat, and insurance bills. It was an astronomical loss for us. For people like Johnny, though, this was a windfall. He stopped paying rent almost immediately after moving in and decided he didn't need to keep his job as an auto mechanic either. His side businesses—dealing drugs and running prostitution—were enough to keep him afloat now that rent was off the table.

We started an eviction process in 2020, but it mattered little. Over the next three years, we faced Johnny in court repeatedly, each time running into new governmental rules that allowed him to continue living rent-free. Eventually, Johnny got the government to cover most of his back rent, as he would slow-pay for a while, stop again, and repeat the cycle. Meanwhile, complaints rolled in from neighboring tenants about his activities, but little could be done.

At one point, after we won an eviction case, Johnny used a loophole in the 2019 Tenant Protection Act to stay in the apartment by paying a partial rent balance. As a result, he couldn't be evicted, his rent couldn't be raised for months, and he avoided paying late fees. And so, the cycle continued.

I'll admit, there were times I wondered whether I should blame Johnny or the system he's learned to work so well. Ultimately, I blame both, in part. Johnny's story is a cautionary tale for real estate investors: tenant screening is your first line of defense. Mistakes, coupled with external challenges like a pandemic, can compound into major losses. Professional tenants can wreak havoc on your property, other tenants, and your management team.

That said, Johnny's case also took a massive amount of my personal time. It was a tough lesson, but I learned from it. And while it's easy to focus on the losses, it's also worth considering the broader impact. How many good tenants may now be screened out because of lessons learned from Johnny? Mistakes like these ripple outward, contributing to challenges like the housing crisis and the lack of affordable rent. Some of that is on local governments, but much of it stems from errors I've since corrected.

Tenant Applications Checklist: Best Practices for Screening

- Date of Birth (DOB), Not Age: Collect DOB rather than age to avoid potential discrimination issues.
- Contact Information: Require email, work email, primary phone, secondary phone, emergency contact, emergency contact email, and emergency contact phone.
- Cosigner Option: Including a cosigner can provide additional financial security.
- Minimum Income Requirements - Establish minimum income requirements at the unit level. Be mindful of discrimination laws regarding income sources. However, states have yet to address situations where tenants cannot afford the unit on paper.
- Job History Verification - Contact employers,

companies, and supervisors to verify job history.
- References - Call all references directly—avoid email.
- Verify phone numbers and confirm the identity of the references.
- Prior Landlord Checks - Contact the current landlord and the one before that. Verify listed landlords against property tax records to ensure the applicant is listing the actual property owner during the stated rental period. Be cautious: current landlords might provide overly positive references to encourage tenants to move out.
- Application Accuracy Statement - Include a clear statement in the application:
  "If you provide false information on this application, it will result in automatic rejection and could be grounds for lease termination."
  (Note: Enforcement of this clause may vary by state and might not hold in court, but it establishes your intent.)

This structured approach helps safeguard against unreliable tenants while maintaining compliance with fair housing laws.

What happens when you can't foresee tenants' issues or when those issues are caused by the management or the owner? We make mistakes. We're managing people and buildings, and the people doing this work have their own flaws too. The answer is simple: we just own those mistakes. If I wait too long to address pests or if someone on my management team fails to screen tenants properly, we correct the issue and move on. But we take responsibility for it, and we expect the same from our tenants.

I view our tenant base very much like I view our staff. Each provides similar services to our business, don't they? If I think of a tenant as an employee, I know that I've agreed to respect them, and in turn, they should respect me. I expect that respect, but it isn't in the lease.

CHAPTER 19

Single Family Houses

As a safe bet, I'm going to assume you want to grow your business beyond ten units. If you don't, no problem, but you still may want to maximize your time, effort, and expenses on the way up to ten. Even if you have one or no rentals, knowing how to efficiently get from point A to point B will help you reach your real estate investment goals.

If you're going to manage properties yourself, you can save a lot of money on expenses and management fees. After reading Mike Butler's book, *Landlording on Autopilot*, where the author outlines basic systems that can be applied across a large number of houses, I knew that single-family homes were certainly going to be a portion of a great real estate portfolio. From the management perspective alone, plain old rental houses are amazing. Self-managing a portfolio of single-family rentals (SFRs) is very do-able, even for the hands-off landlord.

An SFR portfolio allows you to avoid time-consuming tasks like snow removal, landscaping, and utility management. This is because your lease for a traditional SFR will typically require the tenant to handle most of the tasks a landlord would need to manage in a building with common or shared areas. The beauty of the SFR is that the tenants often manage themselves in many ways. That was a huge advantage for me as a new investor and landlord. Had I started out with only multifamily properties, I probably would have overburdened myself with lawns, snow removal, and other upkeep. No matter what type of rental you have, though, regular day-to-day maintenance, repairs, and renovations are still necessary. For an SFR portfolio—especially for an owner who is nearby—this is the best-case scenario for a self-managed business. At certain points in the past, I wouldn't have been able to say this, but today, I am confident I could run a portfolio of 50 single-family homes with one full-time assistant and one maintenance person.

The drawback of SFRs is the amount of money per unit you can make. With only one tenant per property, you're usually earning less than you would with larger multifamily properties. The risks are different, too. With only one tenant in a unit, if something goes wrong—such as a tenant stopping payment or a vacancy—100 percent of the income stops. Also, the margins are smaller. Costs for things like furnaces, water heaters, roofs, and large repairs make SFRs riskier on their own than multifamily rentals. Because of these factors, when I was considering this market segment, I didn't want to limit myself to SFRs. One of my first decisions was to look at both SFRs and multifamily properties of up to four units.

In hindsight, was that the correct decision? Let's run the analysis from a portfolio perspective. Today, SFRs make up about 15 percent of my portfolio. For a small-town landlord, the biggest positives of SFRs start with the opportunity to learn how to handle everything—from advertising to screening to collecting rent and scaling—all on your own. As you fix up an SFR, you're learning the most important parts of the processes you'll eventually scale. If you go through this, pay close attention to the details. You're going to be inclined to focus closely on the money, but what many investors fail to see—and what I failed to see—is the impact of time on renovation projects. Here's one example of how I learned to use contractors—and I learned the hard way.

Avalon Andy – Single-Family House Flip

I met Avalon Andy's son, Andy Jr., during a phase of my life when I was trying to help everyone I thought needed help. These weren't necessarily people who asked for help, but Andy Jr. did. And I accepted. Andy Jr. was struggling with personal issues I had experience with. He was a really smart kid but very lost. After he called me late one night, I phoned another friend, and we went over to try to help him.

When we arrived at the location, there didn't seem to be a house there. After a while, I called him, and he said he was inside. I was confused—inside where? I told him I thought we were in the wrong place. All I saw was an overgrown vacant lot. He said he would come out. A few moments later, I heard rustling in the bushes. Amazingly, Andy was climbing out of a window of a house I didn't even realize was there. The trees and bushes were so overgrown that they completely hid the structure. He stumbled out, and we tried to get him some help. He desperately needed professional help, but like so many others, he wasn't ready.

A couple of years later, after I decided to become a real estate investor, I learned about something called "driving for deals." It's a time-intensive process if you're doing it seriously, but I started casually, during my regular drives through town. The idea is to look for houses that seem neglected—unkempt yards, peeling paint, or other signs of distress. The best opportunities are in nicer neighborhoods where no one is taking care of a property. These homes are often owned by absentee landlords, mismanaged, or caught up in financial trouble due to divorce, taxes, or unpaid mortgages.

On this particular day, I had mapped out a route to proactively look for distressed properties. My aim was to find single-family homes (SFRs) in middle-value neighborhoods—no multifamilies. I was specifically looking for a flip house or a rental. The neighborhood I chose that day was one I used to live in before moving to a larger home. I still owned my first house there, so it was familiar, but I didn't know every block. As I drove down one street, I recognized the old vacant lot from years ago. "Oh yeah," I said to myself. "That's the one with the hidden house!"

It took some effort to locate the owner, but I kept at it. I used public records, which were accessible online thanks to a website I had learned about during a previous house search. Back then, my real estate agent, John, had shown me the site for its flood zone overlays. I looked up the property and found the owner's name. Then I searched for the owner's addresses on Google and sent handwritten yellow letters to all the likely matches. About two weeks later, I got a phone call. It was the owner. Wow—this really works!

I introduced myself as a local investor interested in single-family homes. I told him I wanted to make an offer on his house and asked if he could tell me about it. For the next fifteen or twenty minutes, he told me the entire history of the house—who had lived there and why it was in its current state. These stories are often sad, and this one was no exception. My old friend Andy Jr., whom I had lost touch with, had grown up in that house. When I had seen him there years ago, he was likely squatting. I realized this after piecing together information about the utilities being off and the water bills stopping.

The house and the families who lived there had a history of illness and financial hardship, but there were also good times, according to the owner. Still, I could tell that talking about it was painful for him. It felt like I was asking him to reopen old wounds. I felt bad and wondered if I was doing the right thing.

There was always an ethical struggle I felt when making low offers on distressed real estate. Everything I read and heard told me it was the right thing to do, but on some deals, I just couldn't. I know that's not par for the course, and it's probably not what most homebuyers would tell you, but that's the reality. I needed to sleep well at night, and if I felt like I was ripping off someone vulnerable—like an elderly seller or someone mentally unstable—I walked away from the deal. I didn't want to take advantage of people.

In several cases, when I realized the seller and I weren't going to find common ground, I'd share my analysis of their property and suggest they call my friend John, a realtor. That way, they'd have a better chance of getting what they deserved from the sale, John would get a referral as thanks for his advice to me, and I wouldn't waste time on deals I couldn't or shouldn't get at a discount. Some might disagree with the "shouldn't" part, but I don't. Doing the right thing in business always pays off tenfold.

As for missed opportunities, sure, I knew other investors would probably buy the deals I left behind. That's fine. I used to think there was a shortage of deals. There isn't. There's a shortage of hard work. If you work hard, you'll find the deals.

When it came to the deal, I knew that house would sit there until it rotted away if I didn't step in. The county would spend a fortune foreclosing, take ownership, and let it sit for a year before selling it at auction. Why wait? Why give the open market a chance when I had already done the legwork to find the owner and make the deal? Maybe the owner could've gotten more money by listing it with a realtor, but he hadn't done that in years and was unlikely to start now. Where were those hardworking realtors anyway? Why hadn't they found Andy? I stopped asking those questions a long time ago. Just get the deal. If not you, someone else will.

Andy was paying just enough taxes to stave off foreclosure, but it was money out of his pocket with no return. He didn't have the resources—time, money, or willingness—to renovate the house. While the property needed significant work, I estimated it could've been made rentable with $10,000 and a month's effort. Maybe that was optimistic—the house was hidden behind overgrown bushes, practically invisible from the road. Either way, Andy couldn't handle it, and the unpaid taxes would eventually catch up with him. When that happened, he'd lose everything. We both knew it. What I offered him was better than his other options: I covered the back taxes, all closing costs, and threw in a few thousand dollars for him to pocket. He suggested the number, and I accepted.

Then I learned why he hadn't sold the house sooner: his ex-wife.

God bless her, but Avalon Andy's ex-wife was deeply troubled. Meeting her made it clear that she was struggling significantly with her mental health, and she seemed to lack the support she needed. While I often use humor to cope with difficult situations, I do have a tendency to get emotionally involved in these kinds of scenarios. Some might say that's a flaw in business, and maybe they're right. But having spent years in the selfish, self-centered vortex of addiction, I've gained a different perspective. Surviving that experience gave me the ability to feel deeply again, and I choose not to numb those feelings—whether with substances or with rationalization and justification, as many people do.

When I met Avalon Andy's ex-wife before closing, it was clear she was troubled. I had to come to terms with that, which I did, and we moved forward with the deal. Her mental state wasn't a dealbreaker, but I knew that if they didn't sell me the house, they'd lose everything they didn't even realize they had.

On closing day, things got complicated. The lawyer asked for her license. She didn't have one. He asked for any form of ID. She didn't have that either. We had to delay the closing while she went to the state to get a new license. Eventually, we closed the deal. To my surprise, when the lawyer asked Avalon Andy who to make the checks out to, he directed all the proceeds to his ex-wife. I didn't know enough about their history to understand why, but I was proud of him.

The only problem? Now I owned a lot with an unrecognizable house on it.

Avalon Renovation

The Avalon renovation project is a textbook example of

how to do almost everything wrong. At the time, I wasn't a seasoned investor—I was really just winging it. When I bought Avalon, I decided to make it a flip. I thought I had purchased it at a good enough price that I could invest a significant amount of money into renovations and still leave room for a solid profit. I followed the 70 percent rule, which says that the purchase price plus renovation costs should not exceed 70 percent of the property's after-repair value (ARV). Based on those calculations, I had about $60,000 for renovations, so I got started.

Unfortunately, I didn't take the first critical step: creating a project scope. At the time, I didn't even have a Project Scope Template. I developed that document only after completely botching the Avalon job. It's a simple spreadsheet that covers every area of a property, beginning with the exterior and moving through walls, paint, mechanicals, electrical, HVAC, and anything else you might consider fixing. The template is broad and comprehensive enough for any residential renovation, whether it's a simple paint-and-carpets house flip or a more complex apartment turnover. Using the template has given me a systematic, step-by-step approach to even the most complicated projects.

Avalon wasn't insanely complicated, but it turned out to be a much bigger job than I had anticipated. Did I get a home inspection? "Nah…Dave Drew doesn't need home inspections. He knows everything!" That was my attitude back then. In reality, I knew almost nothing. I went about the entire project backward, making mistakes that could have been avoided with proper planning.

The lessons I learned from single-family renovation failures were so painful that I consider them the best education I ever paid for—and they cost about the same as college!

The Downside of Single-Family Houses

Single-family rentals are excellent in many ways, but they have their downsides. One of the biggest challenges I encountered, as highlighted in the Avalon experience, was spending time on things I didn't need to learn. I invested energy into tasks that I should have contracted out to more qualified professionals. In my effort to save money, I wasted it. In my effort to save time, I wasted it. And in my effort to make a boatload of money, I only made a small shipload. Boo hoo, right? But still, I was lucky.

Did I need to learn flooring, plumbing, and electrical work firsthand to become a successful investor? Definitely not. If I had focused my time on finding great deals and relied on capable property managers, I could have scaled up to larger multifamily properties—or closed more SFR deals—much sooner. I second-guess this decision often, but I always come back to one thing: knowing how to manage every aspect of a rental property gave me the skills to choose great managers. Without that knowledge, I wouldn't have been able to reach the next level.

The truth is, without excellent property management, my business would have failed long ago. The great fact for me remains: you can't succeed without it. Remember, no matter how bad it seems or how many times you feel like banging your head against the wall, it doesn't matter if you fail. What matters is that you get back up and keep going.

Investment Numbers for Single-Family Rentals

Let's look at the actual numbers for SFR investments. Average home prices have risen significantly over the years. Following the 2008 recession and COVID in 2020, the average single-family home sold for about $400,000 in 2023. That's a daunting price point for real estate investors interested in single-family rentals. However, these numbers vary widely depending on location. In Pennsylvania, the average is closer to $230,000; in California, it's about $750,000. In some panhandle states, you can find average home sales at $200,000 or less.

These averages, however, include everything from multimillion-dollar mansions to dilapidated shanties. Most investors don't purchase at retail prices. Instead, we look for deep discounts and value-add opportunities. For example, you could buy a $200,000 house, rent it for $1,500 a month, and still see a great return. That said, you'd likely need substantial cash upfront to make it happen.

With mortgage rates at a twenty-five-year high at the time of this writing, the rising rental rates help offset those costs. A skilled real estate investor can make money in any market if they play their cards right.

For a buy-and-hold strategy with an SFR in New York in 2023, you'd typically aim for a 1 percent monthly return on the purchase price. This means you'd rent a $200,000 house for $2,000 a month. For SFRs, where maintenance costs are lower, your required return doesn't need to be as high as the 2 percent target typically used for multifamily properties.

There are many markets throughout the country very similar to upstate New York, where you can still find $50,000 homes with renovation budgets of $20,000–$30,000, allowing you to rent them for $1,500 per month. These 3 percent deals remain my favorites. With a low barrier to entry, they offer excellent potential for strong returns.

CHAPTER 20

Development

Through interaction with other investors and the extensive learning I gained over ten years of real estate investing, a seed was eventually planted. I was intrigued by Real Estate Development almost as soon as I got into investing. Developing real estate projects always seemed like the next level up from owning and managing rental apartments. I had already gained experience with several facets of development, but my strengths were primarily focused on house flipping, basic renovations, and property management. I went to work. I started learning all I could: books, podcasts, and lots of discussions with developers.

Experience and hard work pay off. Without realizing it, I had built a reputation that would culminate in my earning a role in a multimillion-dollar deal. Overnight, it seemed as though I had reached the next step in my real estate career. Development had always been an ambition, and getting into it required that I quickly begin to sharpen my focus. I used to think I had to clean the toilets to be a successful real estate investor—until I realized I didn't. I felt I had to lay the floors myself—until I didn't. And I believed development had to wait until I was completely comfortable—until I wasn't. One of my goals is to gain wisdom by learning from the experiences of others. If you are interested in real estate development, keep reading, and I'll share the basics of what I learned during my first development project. These are all things I learned the hard way as I endured literally hundreds of sleepless nights. I don't wish that on anyone.

Negotiating multimillion-dollar real estate deals is different from buying $50,000 houses, but the feeling I get when I find a gem is the same. Experienced matters because experts can trust their gut. Novices gamble. With my time in the industry, I knew I could trust mine. I was the local *We Buy Houses* guy, now thinking bigger.

For small-time investors, big deals can seem out of reach. But the approach is the same—assess value, identify revenue streams, estimate costs, and negotiate terms. I won't pretend my motivations were purely noble, but at this stage in my life, I've learned that doing the best for the most people pays dividends beyond money. I followed my own formula and began tackling the belief. This was easy. Lots of people were developers, and real estate development was happening all around my locale. I'd wanted to develop for years. What I needed to do was make a decision. So, I went for a run.

Development deals can come with lower risks and fewer barriers to entry, but many also come with challenges that are significantly more perilous. Bigger deposits, more accountable time frames, and a lot more unknowns than you may encounter compared to a "paint and carpet" renovation like the ones I was really good at. As I ran, I wrestled with doubt. Was I charging ahead or running away? Was this ego, or was there a real opportunity to do something meaningful in this space? Could I have a positive impact on the community and maybe play a part in changing its trajectory? Was there a larger calling attached to the prospect of real estate development than I could see? Was my "why" noble and attainable?

The creativity was flowing and so was the adrenaline. Looking back on that day, I already knew the answers. They were the same answers to every other question I ever asked myself that were shrouded in fear. Of course, you *can* do it, and you *should*! Life presents us with these moments, and in the real time of it all, I felt like I was at a turning point. Would I take the risks or spend the rest of my life wondering if I could have? By the end of my run, my mind was clear. I was in!

With a project size that was ten times anything I'd ever done, there seemed to be extra zeroes on all of these numbers! One of the challenges I encountered was determining what fit into the community. This took coordination with other investors, local officials, and marketing firms. To ensure the deal is successful, exploring options such as tax incentives, grant money, and funding programs was necessary. The information was coming at me like a firehose, but it was exciting. One thing that quickly became clear was that at each new development stage, the mind-blowing cost I'd have to cover would mean I'd have to have or have access to a lot of upfront money. I'll cover the biggest upfront cash costs in a bit.

Another primary challenge in a development project is to figure out what the vision is and how to either convert or redevelop the space. If you are going to become a developer my first piece of advice is this: Try to determine how much time and money the project will take. Then quadruple that. The time is what I really underestimated. My first development deal took 18 months to close!

During those 18 months, I heard that little voice many times again… *Are you sure about this? What if it fails? What will people say?* Doubt plays tricks. It makes you worry about what others think, people who have no experience in what you're doing. Over time, I've learned that most people don't believe they can accomplish great things, and they push those doubts onto others. If we listen, their disbelief becomes powerful. Why should I think I can do this if they can't?

Here's the truth: They're wrong.

Most people couldn't even fathom a project like this. They weren't bad people, but they weren't the ones I needed to be listening to. I left those doubts in the dust and sought out a new group of influencers.

I needed to talk to millionaires, developers, and individuals who had completed large transactions. I had already completed a couple of million-dollar transactions, but this was on another level. My experience got me this far, but it wasn't enough. I needed to understand how successful people got to the next level.

So, I worked on my contacts. Every day, I went through my list, looking for local real estate players who had done big deals. I knew a few, but others I had to track down. I made it my goal to set up at least five meetings or calls per week. Before I knew it, my calendar was packed. My investor prospectus wasn't ready yet, but these conversations paved the way. Soon, we'd be talking about money, investment, and partnership.

Analyzing the Knowns…and the Unknowns

Sometimes, you simply don't know what you don't know. Realizing this can be exciting, surprising, or downright terrifying. The best way to approach the unknown is with humility. If you expect to know everything, you'll end up disappointed, scared, and ultimately humbled. But if you treat this as a fact-finding venture, a chance to learn rather than pretending to know, it becomes easier.

When I grasped the amount of work required to develop a financial plan and waterfall development model, I was crushed. It was like finding the most important homework assignment of the semester crumpled up, at the bottom of your backpack, already past due.

Behind the eight ball, sweating, and staring at a mountain of financial modeling ahead, I at least knew what had to be done. I had to become an Excel jockey again. For two weeks, I worked day and night. I loved it, but it was some of the hardest work I'd done in years. The result was what I now consider the ultimate real estate development modeling tool—worth every minute because, like a rental house, it would pay dividends over the long term.

As I built the tool to evaluate changing factors, loan details, cash flows, and forecasts, I had a sinking feeling: more big pieces of this project would have to shift. To take this investment to the next level, we needed to be more professional, more detailed, and more precise. My mindset shifted from *Is this a good deal?*...to...*I know this is a good deal, but can I prove it to others?* Could I demonstrate to investors why it worked—well enough to persuade them to invest hundreds of thousands or even millions of dollars in it? Into me?

The answer was yes. Emphatically, yes. I had to do it. I was in too deep to stop pressing forward. Burnt out and exhausted, I wasn't ready for what came next. In the middle of the due diligence period—already two months in—I underwent two surgeries. Both were successful, and while I lost two weeks of work, I gained the rest of my life. Another great investment.

Before I could present this deal to investors and lenders, I had to work through several stages. There's no single right way to do this, but for me, the first step was to become the smartest person in the room when it came to this deal. At this level, ambiguity translates to investors as higher risk. It scares them. My goal, therefore, was to be prepared for every question with decisive answers.

Having a broad knowledge base stemming from experience as a small real estate investor is excellent preparation for development, but to get to the next level, you cannot rely solely on that. Development investors as a group are different animals from smaller multifamily or turnkey investors. It wasn't an impossible learning curve, but it was steep in part. There were gaps that needed to be addressed and closed. That meant mastering the key metrics that drive large-scale real estate, multifamily, and development projects. Here are the basics:

Internal Rate of Return (IRR)

IRR is one of the most widely used metrics in real

estate development, with ranges for desirable returns typically between 10 to 20 percent, and 15 percent being common. It measures the annualized, time-weighted return on invested equity, taking into account the timing of cash contributions and distributions. One easy way to consider this metric is to think about it as the total percentage of cash flow left once all other expenses and debts are paid, across the entire life of the investment.

Timing is key to understanding the metric. Money received earlier in a deal is more valuable than money received later. This means shorter hold periods tend to show higher IRRs. For example, a deal with a ten-year hold might have an IRR of 16 percent, while the same deal held for three years could have an IRR of 22 percent. However, the longer hold generates a much higher total profit. This is why IRR alone isn't enough to evaluate a deal—it must be considered alongside other factors.

Cash-on-Cash Return (COCR)

The cash-on-cash return measures the annual cash flow an investor receives in relation to their initial cash investment. For rental properties, this is straightforward—cash flow after debt service divided by the cash invested, which includes the down payment, loan points, and closing costs. Anything above 10 percent is typically considered a strong return.

For development deals, COCR is harder to calculate because projects often have extended periods with no cash flow due to construction, permitting, and lease-up. In the deal I was looking at, expectations were that there would be at least three months without revenue. To account for this, we tracked investment periods by month, identifying when the project would stabilize, meaning it was fully leased, generating positive cash flow, and producing returns. Once stabilized, we could calculate an annualized COCR return, helping investors understand when to expect payouts and how those returns would grow over time.

Equity Multiple (EM)

Equity multiple is one of the simplest and most useful real estate development metrics. It measures how much an investor's money is expected to grow over the life of a deal. In other words, if an investor puts in $100k, what would they expect to walk away with when the developer pays them off or when they exit the deal. In this case, equity multiple can vary widely depending on the other terms of the deal but the number to look for is between 1.5 and 2.0. With an equity multiple of 2.0, an investor who put in $100k would end up with $200k, and that would include the original $100k, over the duration of the investment.

Funding Strategy

For the new complex, a two-pronged approach to financing was employed. First, pursue banks and institutional lenders while simultaneously exploring private funding sources. Private funding can be easy to find but tricky to navigate. Some lenders operate as large businesses with structured processes, while others are smaller groups offering capital with minimal red tape.

Each option has pros and cons. Banks and large financial firms typically require full underwriting and extensive documentation, but often offer more competitive rates. Private lenders tend to charge higher loan points but have fewer requirements, like appraisals or credit checks. It all depends on who you're dealing with.

For the conventional lending route, it is advisable to meet with multiple banks and financial institutions to explore your options. Multi-million-dollar deals will involve more person-to-person meetings. One advantage, something discussed earlier in the book, paid off here. Leaning on the work done to develop strong relationships is invaluable, especially for new developers.

In commercial real estate, every player—lenders, investors, contractors—has their ideas about what you should do with your money. The challenge is keeping the project on track while navigating those competing interests. Some lenders may not be a good fit or may not be willing to work with you. Be prepared for rejection.

If your deal is attractive and penciled out, lenders will want to work with you. You may run into more barriers. No matter how much experience in other spaces you have, managing a large construction and development project is likely bigger and more complex than anything you've done before. Developer experience risk was one of my biggest obstacles, and I was upfront about it. How can you say you've done something if you haven't yet? Some would say being this transparent isn't the best approach, but with lenders, I believe in putting all the cards on the table, especially when the cards are going to be turned over eventually. Acknowledging risk showed we understood the project's scope—and that we cared about the lender's position.

Another key aspect of a successful financing strategy is attracting private equity investors, which presented a significant learning curve. I had limited experience with crowdfunding, syndication, or large-scale joint ventures (JVs). I knew enough from an investor's perspective but had never structured a deal myself. Here are a few basics to understand when funding equity for development projects: These deals typically involve two groups:

- General Partner (GP): The deal sponsor, responsible for acquisition, construction, financing, leasing, operations, and ultimately, selling or refinancing the property.
- Limited Partners (LPs): Passive investors who contribute capital but do not participate in management.

Upfront Costs

One of the biggest differences between development deals and standard residential real estate is the sheer scale of upfront costs. I knew the time commitment for development management would be significant, but the money we had to spend *before* closing was staggering. Just to submit an application to the local municipality, we had to prepare a full civil plan. On a multi-acre property with about a dozen buildings, this meant accounting for everything—from parking and lighting to stormwater drainage and accessibility compliance. Because we were converting a campus primarily into residential housing, we also had to include recreation space, electric vehicle charging stations, and detailed plans for the complex's intended use. We requested proposals from engineering firms and waited. Then the first proposal came in: $40,000. I fell out of my chair. I assumed that because we already had many of the original drawings and planning documents, local firms could leverage them to give us a better price. Bad assumption. Worse, I quickly learned that $40,000 covered only the absolute basics of the site plan. I couldn't sleep for days.

Construction Overages

As the project evolved, so did its costs. Everything—from engineering to design to construction—kept going up. Looking back, I realize that what I thought was logical and practical didn't align with how commercial designers, county and town planners, and engineering firms operated. I went in thinking, *just because that's how it's always been done doesn't mean that's how we have to do it.*

Construction is always the biggest variable in a development project. We started with a modest budget, but within two months, it had doubled and then a few months later, it doubled again. Eventually, I had to accept that the system itself made it difficult to save money on construction. What frustrated me most was that I had been running apartment renovations for years, yet the prices we were now seeing for similar work were exponentially higher. This wasn't ground-up construction, but repurposing the college turned out to be more complex than I had expected. What got you here won't get you there, as Steven Covey would say.

Burnout and Rebirth

From the start, the project moved at a relentless pace. If you ever want to test your limits, risk everything by taking on something far bigger than you think you can handle. I was familiar with pushing myself, but I wasn't prepared for what happened after three months of nonstop work.

People had warned me, but I never believed it could happen to *me*. The best way to describe it is like a form of depression. I knew what needed to be done, but I couldn't act. I was busy all day but not productive. The spark that had driven the project was gone, replaced by exhaustion and detachment. Instead of building relationships, the key to success in this business, I was pushing people away. I felt like I was underwater, constantly hit by waves I could no longer duck. Instead of diving beneath them, I was getting slammed by the whitewater, choking on anxiety.

Life doesn't pause just because you take on a project too big for your britches. As I pushed people, they pushed back. For someone who preaches the importance of relationships and a positive attitude, I wasn't living up to my own words. And people started letting me know, my wife most of all.

Things came to a head one night during an argument about something completely unrelated to real estate. I hadn't realized how much I had changed. But when she laid it all out, I felt sick. My demeanor, my attitude, and how I was treating my wife were completely inconsistent with how I felt about her. I was blindsided.

I wasn't holding up my end of the bargain.

For someone who makes deals for a living, I had forgotten the most important one—the deal I made with her when we got married. My real estate project was minuscule compared to *that* deal. And I was failing. I had been dragging my wife, my kids, my partners—everyone I cared about—behind a project that, in the grand scheme of things, didn't matter nearly as much as they did. I was working harder than ever, but the reality was that I was failing at *both* the deal and my life.

Then came the breaking point. The night before a big event, everything caught up with me. The stress, the pressure, the misplaced priorities—it all boiled over. I was hitting bottom, again.

I had been here before, years ago, when I thought my life was over. Back then, the symptoms of the problem had been alcohol and drugs. This time, it looked different—but the basis and the roots were the same. Was I out for the good of the most people and my loved ones, or was I chasing selfish goals again? Was I letting the perceived success of a real estate project blind me to the losses I was chalking up in my personal life? Who knew that self-destruction could be disguised as ambition and good intentions?

The thought of losing my family and wasting the time and money of everyone who had trusted me was unbearable. My pain threshold for this kind of thing is probably higher than most, but even I couldn't take it anymore. The fear of failure, the fear of success, the weight of letting people down—it consumed me. Just when I thought I couldn't handle anything else, life threw me skin cancer and a dislocated shoulder.

I was done.

I stopped.

I got down on my knees and asked for help.

Lying in bed that night, I started thinking about my family. *What if I don't wake up tomorrow? Will they be okay? Have I been the husband and father I should be? If I were gone tomorrow, will I have left anything unfinished?*

And then, as the fear and the dark thoughts crept in, something shifted.

Alone in the dark, I saw my life from another angle. I felt like I was looking down on everything—my whole existence laid out before me. My wedding photos hung on the wall, a reminder of how young and happy we were. Across the room, I saw pictures of me with each of my three boys at their preschool Valentine's Day celebrations. I had been there for them then. I was still here for them now—even if I didn't *feel* it. The reality was, I had lost *nothing*.

I kept looking. My oldest son's baseball uniform hung up, freshly cleaned, grass stains removed. I had coached him for years. Those uniforms kept getting bigger, and they would continue to—*with or without me.*

Whatever had carried me through the hardest times in my life, I realized, was also there for them. Call it faith, a sign, a spiritual awakening—it was all of those things.

And in that moment, I saw it.

I saw the error of my ways.

I saw that I was not the center of the universe.

I saw that the most important things in life had *nothing* to do with real estate development.

A weight was lifted.

I sat in my meditation chair the next day and questioned everything. When I first committed to the deal, I had told myself there was a specific amount I was willing to lose—an amount that would be worth the risk. I thought back to the day on the running trail when I made the decision. By December, ten months later, I had already invested four times that amount.

I kept finding myself at the end of my rope, once again prioritizing the wrong things—spending too much time in my head, consumed by the deal, instead of being present with my wife and kids. I started to cry. *What's the difference?* I thought. *What if I lose it all? Who cares what people say?* Sure, I'd have to explain to people what happened, but eventually, it would pass.

Screw it. Call it a day and move on.

I was done. I surrendered. Again. For real.

The relief was instantaneous. It felt like a million-pound anvil lifted off my chest. I could have floated upstairs to bed. Whenever things like this happen, I call them spiritual awakenings. I've had enough time to recognize my patterns. I only see them clearly in hindsight, but they always involve pushing through fear—sometimes it's quick, other times it's slow.

The year before I took on this project, I had returned from an extended trip abroad, telling myself it was time to simplify my life. Then, almost immediately, I dove into a huge development deal! I wasn't ready for simple yet. Life has a way of reminding you who's boss.

Within two months that year, I was diagnosed with cancer and had surgery. I dislocated my shoulder and had another surgery. I lost my 25-year-old nephew to an overdose. Then my mother died. I kept going through it all. Then, just before I was supposed to close on the sale of one of my apartment buildings that was meant to fund the upfront costs I couldn't afford, it burned to the ground. You cannot make this stuff up. Every day, I asked myself—and whatever force was guiding me—to show me the path. I trudged forward.

The rest is more of the same. History. Eighteen months after the contract was first signed, the deal closed, and an entirely new phase began…actually building the place.

CHAPTER 21

Financial Independence

Defined in a simple real-world context, financial independence means that you are no longer dependent on a job where you make money for someone else's business. It means you are creating your own income and meeting the financial requirements you set for yourself. There's more coming in than going out, and you are cash flow positive. It doesn't mean you don't have to work. While there may be a reality where work is no longer needed, the intrinsic value—the built-in value—of work on a human being can't be forgotten. Work is a core part of who we are. Genetically and socially, humans were shaped through work. It molded us into the race we are today. While the type of work we do and the intensity with which we do it will change, there's always going to be something you need to do to keep going, and this is a good thing.

Humankind is accomplishing feats that were unimaginable only a few years ago, thanks to technological advancements and developments like AI. The world will always be changing. It's going to change faster, and that's not going to stop. Adapting to those changes, while still acknowledging our shared human drives, makes life today during the Technological Revolution look very different than it did for our grandparents.

Financial independence today also looks a lot different. What does financial independence look like to you?

Imagine a world where you have enough money coming in through your investments that you could quit your day job. This was one of my earliest goals, and I achieved it after only a couple of years. Imagine being able to tell your boss that you no longer have to work for that company. Depending on who my boss was at the time, I would imagine different ways to deliver that message—varying tones, phrases, and levels of dramatics. I've had a lot of bosses, so there was no shortage of possibilities. Hopefully, for you, when it comes time to deliver the message, it will look, sound, and feel exactly like what it represents: freedom.

Now imagine not having a boss at all. Picture what you might do with the time you used to spend sitting at your desk or doing whatever else it was that helped make someone else rich. Would you write more? Get in better shape? Spend more time with your family? Look toward greater opportunities.

Be careful when imagining all this, though, because if you're anything like me, all of this could come true—and you still might not end up doing any of those things you're dreaming about.

Financial independence can be a path to using your time more effectively and making more informed decisions. Achieving it requires changing how you think, adjusting your actions, and embracing a bigger mindset. Bigger doesn't always mean more money. It could mean pursuing the things you once thought were impossible or finding ways to be of greater service to others. It may seem more like adjusting your lifestyle to align with your core values. Maybe it's about considering how many people you can help, not just how much you can earn.

Society has taught many of us the lie of "someday" and the myth of retirement. There used to be a reality where working for someone else your whole life was the *only* way to earn what you deserved. But why listen to those outdated rules? Why stay enslaved to the machine? Why conform to a system you already know is antiquated? Through real estate investment – or just with a changed mindset - you can escape the rat race, stand on your own two feet, and focus on the things in life you're passionate about.

Are real estate investment and property management the only way to achieve financial independence? Of course not. Today, I invest in a variety of sectors: stocks, startups, brick-and-mortar businesses, and virtual enterprises. But real estate was always the catalyst—the key. To travel down every financially free road I've ever taken, I needed a vehicle. For me, that vehicle was real estate—and it could be for you too.

After about two years of investing in real estate, working insane hours, and giving it everything I had, something happened. At the time, I was reading Dave Ramsey's *The Total Money Makeover,* and I started tracking my net worth instead of focusing solely on my income. Because I was buying houses and buildings at deep discounts, fixing them up, and renting them out, I didn't realize how much my equity was growing. My bank account was often low—it always was—but my net worth must have been growing, right? I had no idea, so I decided to put it all into a spreadsheet to track the trend.

What I discovered brought a wave of emotion over me. I began to cry. The realization came after two years of relentless focus on real estate and a 10x amount of hustle. I still had my 9-to-5 job so my days often started before 5 a.m. and went late, sometimes until 11 p.m. It was an unsustainable pace, but I always kept going. Those first two years were exhilarating in many ways, but I'll never forget the night I came up from my basement office, the place where I had toiled for countless hours crunching numbers, closing deals both on and off paper, and working toward achieving financial independence. After I saw it, I walked upstairs to find my wife. We only had a few thousand bucks in the bank at the time, but I said, "Honey, guess what? I think we are millionaires!"

A New Perspective

Never have we been in this moment. It's always brand new. The trick is remembering it will always change. Gratitude helps keep focus on what matters most. I try to help others. I try to stay grounded. Nothing I gain is ever truly mine to keep—whether it's money, work, or life itself. It all passes. Staying present and learning to enjoy life hasn't come naturally to me. Just like business, life is unpredictable. And eventually, you start wondering what it's all about.

Your experience doesn't have to be the same as mine. Of course, it won't be. I urge you to attempt to relate to it. Think about what rock bottom looks like to you and what you've done to work through that. Think about times when you knew you were beaten but didn't give up. Focus on those wins. Your life is full of them. Your potential is probably far greater than you think. Don't let those mental barriers stand in your way. Don't camp on the side of the mountain; keep climbing.

While your goals may remain, circumstances will keep changing, so you adapt. You adjust, pivot, and move on. Sometimes our goals in life morph right along with whatever is happening in the moment. Versatility will prevail. If you want things to be different, change them. If you can't change them, work on accepting them. Somewhere in the middle is where happiness lives. It's in the process as we navigate the struggle.

Life is fun. An adventure. Exciting. Worth living.

I'll leave you with this. One of my son Jesse's favorite singers is Miley Cyrus. *Don't tell my dad or any of my childhood friends*...but I've always loved one of her songs, "The Climb." There's a line about how there's always going to be another mountain, always another uphill battle. That part sticks with me.

"It's not about how fast I get there. It's not about what's waiting on the other side. It's the climb!"

Acknowledgements

Writing The Small Town Investor has been a transformative journey filled with more lessons than I ever imagined. Like anything in my life that is big, I could not have done it alone.

First, I thank my family who stood by me through the long nights, setbacks, and the constant juggling of work, writing, and real life. Your patience, encouragement, and love gave me the strength to keep moving forward.

I am truly thankful to the mentors and fellow investors who generously shared their knowledge and stories with me. Your insights have helped shape both my business and the lessons in these pages.

To my friends and partners—thank you for reminding me of the importance of balance, laughter, and perspective, especially in the toughest times.

I also owe a huge debt of gratitude to the recovery community, which showed me the power of belief, decisions, and actions—not only in real estate, but in life itself. There are hundreds of people who have contributed to my well-being and growth.

Finally, this book is dedicated to the dreamers in towns of all sizes who wonder if they can break free from the grind. If my journey proves anything, it's that you can.

ABOUT THE AUTHOR

Dave Drew

Dave currently resides in Central NY with his spectacular wife, Diana, and his three fantastic boys, Davey, Colin, and Jesse. Dave loves playing the guitar while watching the sunset and spending time with his family. When he's not chasing after the real estate business, you can find him at the gym, on a baseball field, or in the car (driving his kids all over the place).

Dave had a wonderful experience growing up on Long Island. As a child of the eighties and nineties, big wheels, BMX bikes, Nintendo, and G.I. Joes were all over the place. Summers were filled with beaches, boats, and all kinds of sports. Seeking a change of pace, Dave has lived in a small Upstate NY town for the last 20 years.

One of Dave's greatest joys is travel, which fuels the creative spirit. He would love to see you and talk in a Café somewhere out there in the world. He'll be the one in the Mets hat, sipping a coffee and staring off into the sunset. That look on his face will be one of tremendous gratitude, never forgetting that every single "extra" day he gets is one to be savored.

Live every day to its fullest and like Tim McGraw sings: "Someday I hope you get the chance… to live like you were dyin'!"

www.ingramcontent.com/pod-product-compliance
Lightning Source LLC
Chambersburg PA
CBHW050905160426
43194CB00011B/2301